Fit For A King

A Short History of Yorkshire's Wool Industry and Trade

Revel Barker

P
Palatino Publishing

First published in in 2021 by Palatino Publishing.
Copyright © Revel Barker 2021

By the same author:
Alternative History
> *The Hitler Scoop*

Fiction
> *The Mayor of Montebello*
> *The Magistrate of Montebello*
> *The Blood Secret*

Non– fiction
> *The Last Pub In Fleet Street*
> *Field Of Vision*
> *Crying All The Way To The Bank*
> *The First Gozitans (... and Ġgantija)*

Fit For A King
A Short History of Yorkshire's
Wool Industry and Trade
ISBN: 978-1-907841-18-7

The moral right of the author has been asserted in accordance with the Copyright, Designs and Patents Act, 1988.

No part of the publication may be reproduced, stored or transmitted in any form or by any means without the prior permission in writing of the publishers.

Palatinobooks@gmail.com

Revel Barker, son of a tailor, was born half-way between Leeds and Bradford and started writing for newspapers while still at school. He worked, first, for the *Pudsey and Stanningley News*, and joined the *Yorkshire Evening Post* in Leeds at 17 – becoming the youngest staff reporter that newspaper had ever employed.

He joined the *Daily Mirror* before his 21st birthday and spent ten years covering the northern counties before moving to London and the *Sunday Mirror* where he became defence correspondent and foreign editor, covering several wars and rounding the globe half a dozen times.

A new publisher, Robert Maxwell, appointed him editorial adviser and then group managing editor and director of Mirror Colour Print.

After taking early retirement from the newspaper industry he became a director and later a consultant for two UK universities.

In 2021 he was elected a Fellow of the Royal Historical Society.

*And was Jerusalem buildèd here,
Among these dark Satanic Mills?*
(William Blake, 1804)

View over Kirkstall Road, Leeds, 1950s
Yorkshire Evening Post

Contents

Acknowledgements and sources
Dedication
PART ONE
  Biggest and Best   11
  The King's New Clothes   19
  The Merino   30
  Counting Sheep   31
  Just Wool   34
  A King's Ransom   39
  Spinning A Yarn   42
  The King's Tax On Sacks   44
  Get Weaving   49
  On Tenterhooks   61
  Edward, Wool King   65
  Reformation   73
  Boom Time for Looms   78
  The Maister   91
  Dyeing for the Country   101
  A Parliament of Owls   106
  Cloth Halls   114
  Worsted Revolution   124
  Transport   135
  Canals and Coaches   141
  Industrial Revelation   145

Revolution	149
Luddites	155
Satan's Seat	167
Steam Power	174
The Factory System	179
Vertically Challenged	182
Dark Satanic Mills	185
Reform	197
Master and Man	210
Railway Lines	219
Rise and Rise	223
The Giants	226
Panic	234
Labour Relations	242
Rise and Fall	248
Worstedopolis	256

PART TWO

A Prince of Wales Check	261
Ready-to-Wear	271
2020 Vision	281
A Personal Postscript	289
Glossary	296

Acknowledgements and Sources

Credit for the genesis of this book is due, in no small part, to my Rawdon friend Ron Brown who told me the (at first, seemingly unlikely) story of Samuel Marsden, of the first shipment of Merino wool, and of a suit length of it being woven for King George III on a hand-operated loom in a mill complex that had once included Ronnie's house.

There were several references to it in the Bradford evening paper, the *Telegraph and Argus*, but none in any book that I could find, and I eventually backtracked the story from historical papers in Australia, and then, via the confident confirmation of A W Hainsworth & Sons in Stanningley, right back to William Thompson's loom in Rawdon. Along the way I found books about mills in Yorkshire, but no book about the history of one third of the county being the wool merchandising, weaving and tailoring centre of the world. Hence this one.

I am especially grateful to my old friend (Dr) James Mahoney, not only for his own family's agricultural interest and knowledge but also for his enthusiastic and skilful guidance through the many Australian National Library archives in Canberra.

Some sadly defunct operations – notably the Halifax Piece Hall and the Sunny Bank Mills in Farsley – retain archivists who were particularly helpful; I am still waiting to hear from several local authority frontmen who promised to call me back.

Finally, I should add that, as a constant reader, I find copious references to footnotes, endnotes or chapter notes both irritating and intrusive, often forcing a pause part-way through a sentence to check a source or explanation. For this reason alone (it is not a thesis written for a degree) I have generally avoided references to sources other than where I think it might help to colour the plot. In some cases sources are directly referenced within the text; in most others I think they are either irrelevant or obvious. (There is a glossary at the back.)

Among literature I consulted, before writing, were:

> Hakluyt, *Collection of Voyages* (1436)
> Henry Best, *Rural Economy* (1641)
> Ralph Thoresby, *Ducatus Leodiensis*, (1715)
> Paul de Rapin, *The History Of England* (1724)
> Daniel Defoe, *A tour thro' the whole island of Great Britain* (1724-1727)
> Arthur Young, *A Six Months' Tour through the North of England* (1770)
> John Luccock, *Observations on British Wool* (1800)
> Statistical Society of London *Journal(s)* (1800s)
> John James, *History of the Worsted Manufacture in England* (1857)
> The Yorkshire Post, *Leeds And Its History* (1926)
> Ruth Strong, *The Hainsworth Story* (2006)
> George Ingle, *Trouble At T'Mill* (2013)
> Susan Duxberry-Neumann, *Little Germany* (2015)
> Paul Chrystal, *Bradford At Work* (2018)
> Richard Morris, *Yorkshire* (2018)

Wikipedia was a great help in finding original source material and most of the illustrations in the book were mined from it as in the public domain. If I have infringed any copyright it was accidental, and I will be pleased to hear about it and make any amendments.

Spinning, carding, combing, and weaving wool
Italy, 1374

This book is dedicated to the fond memory of my friend
Ernest Boyes who gave me my first suit length of
Yorkshire-made worsted.

My days are swifter than a weaver's shuttle.
Book of Job. 7:6.

Biggest and Best

God's Own County... even those sad people, who have never visited it, know which one it is. The ill-informed may dismiss it as a land of flat caps and whippets, where blokes work down t'pit and lasses work in t'mill, and some of those perceptions may be (or may once have been) at least partly true. But the other side of the coin is that it was, and is, widely considered to be the most beautiful of all the counties, by far the biggest in size and certainly the greatest in self-regard.

'The Englishman's Texas': so big, they named it thrice, and then had to divide it later into four, just to manage the place.

There could be only three 'Ridings', because the word came from the Norse: *thriding*, or thirding – north, east, and west – all of them meeting at the city of York.

The North Riding had England's green and pleasant land, from the rough Pennines and the Lake District across majestic peaks and valleys, (nowadays including three national parks that occupy 40% of the county acreage), to the cliffs of Ravenscar, 600 feet above the North Sea, plus Scarborough and Whitby. The East Riding had ecclesiastical Beverley and the seaside resorts of Bridlington and Hornsea and the important trading port of Hull on the Humber: the confluence of the rivers Hull, Ancholme, Derwent, Ouse and Trent.

The West Riding was where the work was done to support the rest of the county — and also the rest of the country – and to make Yorkshire, if anybody wanted to argue about the fact, more sustainable and deserving of independent status within the United Kingdom than, say, Scotland.

Yet a thirding was not the end of the partition. Within, and skirting, the West Riding were the subdivisions of which the Wool District (basically around Leeds and Bradford, but including Skipton, Wakefield Huddersfield and Halifax) was the biggest and most important – not only to Yorkshire, but to the whole of the kingdom, even before the kingdom became 'united' – and which would have within it the Heavy Woollen District, as well as separate White Cloth, Coloured Cloth and Mixed Cloth areas.

Then there were parts of the Riding separately devoted to worsteds, or woollens, or felt, velvet or kersey, or carpets, or working with flax, and others, usually dotted around on the edge of the worsted districts, making blankets. (All of that, without even stopping to consider coal, iron, steel and glassmaking.)

Although there would become an impression that wool was a Yorkshire product and cotton a Lancastrian one, there were some weavers in the west of the West Riding concentrating, like their brethren at the other side of the Pennines, on cotton: and some weavers of wool in Manchester, and yet others experimenting with weaving a mixture of cotton and wool, or mohair and wool, or silk and wool.

Wool textile production was geographically based: fine worsted for suit cloth in Huddersfield; worsted, silk and velvet in Bradford; shoddy and mungo in Dewsbury and Batley; carpets in Halifax. All of them employing the same skill-set – of carders, combers, spinners, weavers, dyers, burlers and finishers – all working to a different end. Mill towns had set their individual preferences which would change little over 300 years.

In other words, although the external perception of the West Riding may have been that they were all doing the same thing (producing and weaving wool), lots of them were doing different things, and doing those things in different ways and, importantly, often with quite differing levels of quality.

Technically, anything made of wool is 'woollen', but within the industry and trade there are some vital distinctions, and they depend on how the same product (wool) is treated. Worsted fabric – for gentlemen's fine suiting and ladies' costumes and skirts – is called 'stuff'; all other woollen material, indeed, all the other stuff such as blankets, overcoats, uniforms, tweeds, and even carpeting, is called 'cloth'.

Wool is known to have been spun and woven into cloth in Pudsey during the bronze age (3000BC to 1200BC).

There was nothing peculiar about spinning and weaving; it took place everywhere in England where there were sheep, and there were sheep everywhere in England. But nowhere were there more sheep in England than in the hills, dales, moors, and valleys, gouged out by glaciers and erosion from the rapidly running rivers, streams and becks of Yorkshire.

Every Yorkshire village had its own identifying traditions and its unique and distinctive area, usually marked out with (often disputed) boundary posts, and residents would 'beat the bounds', processing around their claimed territory once a year, a ceremony that in some cases took two days to complete. They 'kept themselves to themselves', their realms developing (or dwindling) according to their own initiative and intelligence, or stagnating, due to ignorance. Villages may have been within easy walking distance, and within sight, of each other but – with the exceptional necessity that, as farmers, they knew about avoiding inbreeding – they had little or no external social intercourse. (And even then, a father might ask a son who announced his intention of marrying a girl coming from a neighbouring village: 'What's wrong with her, if lads in her own village don't want her?')

In the Yorkshire woollen patois every letter T in that last, quoted, sentence would, more than likely, have been dropped; for another form of division was in speech.

Just as the Yorkshire dialect (as a whole) differed from that of Lancashire, so did that of Bradford (where the first letter D is silent) from Leeds, which it adjoins, or Skipton from Keighley, or Ilkley from Otley. The weavers met their neighbours at the cloth halls and markets, but otherwise did not integrate. They each had their own village customs, their own cricket and football teams, their own brass bands and choirs and, when wealthy mill-owners decided it would be advantageous to educate the masses by teaching them to read and learn about machinery, their own mechanics' institutes and libraries.

It was probably this very native stubbornness, this disinclination to communicate, that held back the progress of weaving in the wool industries when they started.

For the fact is that, from the time of the Romans to the early 1800s, the pattern of weaving in Yorkshire would hardly change.

In the winter of 1069-70, the Norman Conqueror, in his immediate 'harrying of the north' to prevent Saxon rebellion, laid waste to most of Yorkshire. Entire villages were razed and their inhabitants killed, livestock was captured or slaughtered and stores of food destroyed or stolen.

The *Domesday Book* (1086) would record Leeds (*Ledes*) as having 36 households: 27 villagers, four smallholders, four freemen, and a priest. Leeds also had 14 ploughs and one mill – for grinding corn.

York had one church, but no recorded population.

Wakefield (*Wachefeld*) was partially waste, but was populated by 9 villagers, 11 freemen, 22 smallholders, and 3 priests.

Halifax did not make it into the book. Perhaps its compilers could not cope with the treacherous tracks they would need to follow to reach and assess it.

West of Leeds, Bradford (abandoned settlements, no recorded population) was a green bowl in the foothills of the Pennines with one broad fording (hence its name) across one of the becks that ran into the River Aire. Like Leeds it was part of the domain of the De Lacy family (from Lassy in Calvados, Normandy) but 20 years after the invasion, and following the northern harrying, Bradford was still dismissed, as were most villages, like Pudsey, as 'wasteland'.

However, 'waste', in this context, does not mean that the land so described was useless or worthless: it indicates that it was under–populated or uninhabited. It is not inconceivable that the Yorkshiremen were aware when the vengeful and destructive army was on its way, and sought sanctuary among the remote moors and dales, until it had passed.

Farsley (*Ferselleia*), for example, was also listed as a 'settlement', but with no inhabitants to record. Skipton (*Sciptone*) was yet another 'settlement' – apparently with no people visibly settled within it.

Similar disappearing action may have been taken when the Scots army raided and plundered the northern counties, killing anybody they found, shortly after William's army had returned to the south. It may not be so surprising, then, that almost the entire region, north and west of Leeds and Wakefield, was dismissed in 1086 as being 'waste'.

The De Lacys were given West Yorkshire (and land in Lincolnshire and part of Lancashire) as a reward for supporting William the Bastard in his 1066 victory at Hastings. They would build an impressive castle at Pontefract ('broken bridge') but more importantly they would support the building of great abbeys, notably at

Kirkstall, Bolton, Fountains (so named because of the number of natural springs around it) and at Rievaulx in the Rye Valley. And the monks there would breed, rear, and shear sheep. The local farmers and householders were already doing the same. In Saxon Britain, milk for cheese, an important source of winter protein, was the main product of sheep, with wool and meat originally being merely valuable by-products. When a ewe was too old to produce milk, it was fattened for slaughter. It was what Yorkshire's broad acres were best suited for: far better than for corn or for cows.

The Conqueror had brought many people from Flanders with him, and they were given land by him. Their entourage would have included a weaver and a tailor or two; after all, a conquering army would need a change of clothing after its bloody battles – and it might be reasonable to assume that the Norman families would remain sufficiently well suited.

The surname Fleming (meaning 'from Flanders', already an industrious area of western Europe) was fairly common under Norman rule: William the Fleming owned Wath-on-Dearne in the late 1200s, and a couple of Flemings were later mayors of York, where Giles of Brabant would be bailiff in 1308. Maurice de Gant (or Ghent) was, in 1207, first Lord of the Manor of Leeds. John of Gaunt, brother of the Black Prince, had (as his anglicised name implies) been born in Ghent.

It is most likely that the invaders would – if they had not already discovered it – have worked out a better quality of clothmaking, separating long, straight sheep fleeces from the short and rough hairs, to make a finer form of material, and that this imported knowledge would eventually spread widely across the country.

A couple of hundred years later it would acquire a name: worsted.

Country folk may have been clothed thanks to the local sheep man or his neighbours – most shepherd families possessed a loom – but the rest of the population would buy on a market stall garments that most closely fitted them, which were almost certainly imported from countries to which their raw wool, straight off the sheep, had been sold.

Yorkshire folk were always quick at learning but remarkably slow at innovation.

It would not be until about 1770 – when weaving was still a wholly cottage-based occupation – that they would come to the fore. The West Riding would start to overtake and dominate the industry, improving both the quality of its weaving and of its tailoring. And within a few years its clothiers would be suiting the world's nobility – its kings, queens and emperors, its kaisers and tsars, its princes and princesses, its archdukes, dukes and duchesses, and also their armies. And their subjects.

And England's kings and queens, and kings-in-waiting, would be steering what would become the Riding's industry, from wool–trading and weaving, to fashion and tailoring.

The King's New Clothes

Samuel Marsden was born in 1765, only son and the eldest of eight children of a farmer in Farsley, a small settlement in Airedale, where he attended the village school. At 14 he went to work in his uncle's smithy, across the Aire in Horsforth, where he was somehow recruited by an Anglican evangelical group, who sent him, first, to Hull Grammar school and from there to Magdalene College, Cambridge, which he left in 1792 without taking a degree. The following year he was ordained and sent as a missionary to the penal colony in New South Wales, a journey taking more than seven months.

He is possibly nowadays best remembered, south of the equator, as the man who brought Christianity to New Zealand and who also later introduced wine growing and wool to that uncivilised country. A couple of church schools, several streets, a river, a cross, and a coastal point are named there in his lasting honour.

There are worse memories of him in Australia in his

role as Anglican pastor to the early English settlers, most of whom were transported convicts. Within a year of his arrival he was appointed as magistrate and quickly achieved a reputation for excessive sentencing – in some cases, 300 lashes of the cat-o'-nine tails, inevitably baring convicts' flesh to the bone, effectively a death sentence – and also where, unsurprisingly, he became regarded with both fear and contempt as 'the flogging parson'.

The one thing for which he is barely remembered is for being the man who introduced Merino wool to the English (Yorkshire) textile industry and thus deserves great credit for introducing the internationally important Australian wool trade (and giving the West Riding's weavers a terrific advantage in being able to improve the overall quality of their otherwise often indifferent standard of cloth).

Merino sheep had been bred in Spain and meticulously developed over centuries, producing a fleece with long, fine soft strands, creating yarns in great demand by the high-quality textile weavers of Bruges, Ghent and Florence. Before the 18th century exporting any Merinos from Spain had been a crime punishable by death. But in 1790 King Charles IV (in the absence of any other known foreign policy) gave small flocks of them to friendly nations in Europe.

Around 1783-4 the private interests of King George the Third had started to turn towards agriculture. He adapted many of the royal parks into 'farms' for experimental breeding of livestock. He became known as 'Farmer George' and, being well aware of the importance to the country of wool, he kept a particular eye on his sheep flocks.

He had responded to the Spanish gift with 'a set of the finest English' (actually Hanoverian) coach horses, which were highly rated in Europe. He put the Merino sheep out to graze on the pastures around his favourite palace at Kew, where they did not adapt well to a change from the hot-summer-Mediterranean climate of Estremadura, and were noticeably 'more tender' (in need of more attention) than the native stock.

Even shearing them, it was reported to the King, was more difficult, because of the 'extreme greasiness of their fleece which cannot be washed out with cold water'. And, having been sent a sample of their flesh to eat, the message came that 'The King had desired to have no more Spanish mutton at his table'.

Prince William of Holland who, wisely realising that the prevailing weather in Holland was less than ideal for their development, shipped two rams and four ewes to the warmer Dutch colony based around the Cape of Good Hope in south Africa. The governor returned the original flock to Holland when ordered to do so by a new Dutch Republic in 1795, but he had retained their offspring.

There, in 1797, the flock was discovered and, now 26 strong, was offered for sale at £4 a head by the governor's widow – and bought by an entrepreneurial Royal Navy captain, John Waterhouse, commanding HMS *Reliance*, a discovery ship en route to Australia. Space on these vessels was at a premium and the flock had to be accommodated among the officers for the

7,000–mile voyage. Captain John Hunter RN, governor of Australia, wrote that:

> Each officer had, on his own account, given up during the passage the comforts of his accommodation on board and filled them with such animals as their respective cabins were capable of taking in. This, although a private consideration, is nevertheless a public benefit to the colony, and is much to be commended.

After docking in Port Jackson (Sydney) the Merino sheep (now valued at £15 each) were sold to a Captain John Macarthur and to the Rev Samuel Marsden, part-time farmer.

Without any doubt or hesitation, both men had recognised the great quality of the sheep's fleeces.

Marsden first lived in barracks at Parramatta (about fifteen miles inland, now an outer suburb of Sydney). To support and feed his household he had been granted 100 acres of land in the Field of Mars near Dundas — part of Parramatta. He bought 128 acres at South Creek and in 1795, with the help of five convicts assigned to his farms, produced 500 bushels of wheat. The following year he had two mares, two cows, 77 pigs, 49 goats and 16 sheep. Official reports show that there were 1,531 sheep in total in the colony in 1796.

Only a year later – when *Reliance* docked at Port Jackson – Marsden's holdings had expanded to some 3,000 acres, manned by convict labour, accommodating 44 cows, 100 pigs... and 1,000 sheep. (Although at five-pence a fleece, compared with £2 per carcase for meat, there was no inducement to produce wool.)

In 1804, having been sent back to England (three years earlier) to face a court martial for shooting and wounding a fellow officer in a duel, Capt Macarthur had an inspirational idea for developing his small Merino flock – and for creating his own business. He presented his scheme to a friend who introduced him to the Prince of Wales, (the 'Prince Regent') who he clearly impressed. Macarthur was allowed to buy seven rams and two ewes from the King's Merino stud. He then returned to the colony with a commission to establish a wool industry, along with a grant of 5,000 acres of the best pasture land and a guarantee of 5,000 more if tangible results were forthcoming, plus the offer of convicts to work for him. (His court martial for duelling was abandoned after three or four years on the basis that, having happened on the other side of the world, there was a lack of available witnesses.)

However, in 1807, before Macarthur's industry had got off the ground, and without even being aware of it, Marsden the missionary farmer went home to England to report to the Crown on the state of affairs in the colony, taking a barrelful of his own Merino fleeces with him.

He carried it home to Farsley, where Hainsworth's, an established weaving dynasty in the township – still operating today on an impressive scale – recorded that he presented and offered his sample of wool. They had rejected it, being dissatisfied by its quality after a journey halfway round the world in a barrel originally used for shipping wine (or, more likely in those days, rum).

Not discouraged, Marsden simply took his fleeces the short distance across the River Aire to William

Thompson's Low Mill at Rawdon, which, like Farsley, was part of Leeds and on the border of Bradford, where it became the first Merino wool spun and woven in England and from which the pastor had a worsted suit tailored in wool and, appropriately for the missionary's calling, dyed black.

George III

While receiving news and an updated account of the colony, which included a request from Marsden for more clergy and more teachers, King George III – who was clearly not as mad as has been alleged – was reportedly distracted by the quality of the fine new clerical coat that his petitioner was wearing, and asked about it.

It is quite possible that he had been present when George 'Beau' Brummell himself, confronted by the Duke of Bedford wearing a coat of embroidered silk with silver thread and embellished by diamonds, that had cost £500 in 1790 (equivalent to about £28,000 in 2020) had felt the lapel, between forefinger and thumb, and asked, 'Call that thing a coat?'

George III cared about the way people – especially the men busying around him – dressed. In 1798 he had introduced both a 'dress' and a plainer 'undress' uniform of a knee-length coat of dark blue wool worn with white knee–britches and a white waistcoat for male members of the court.

It would survive as formal dress at Windsor until 1936.

The King was so obviously impressed by the soft, fine feel of the vicar's plain black cloth that Marsden promised and delivered him a suit–length of the same wool from the Rawdon mill. The names of the spinner, of the weaver and of the tailor have been lost to time. It is quite likely that William Thompson, being so enthusiastic about the quality of the wool, did the weaving himself. Naturally, the king's favour, along with his gift of five Merinos to take back to Australia from his farm, created great interest among members of the court and a desire for wool coats of a similar quality.

A friend wrote to Marsden from England:

> 'I rejoice heartily in the success of your Merinos: the gift was worthy of the royal donor and cannot fail to be of nearly as much value to the colony as to your self... By cross breeds from these there can be no doubt that your wool, already so fine, will rival if not surpass the best wools in the world...'

Back in the antipodes, Marsden returned to his different flocks. Four years later more than 4,000 lbs (1,800 kg) of his Merino wool was sold in England at 45d a lb. It was the first commercial shipment of any type of wool from Australia, and William Thompson was said to have bought and paid for it in advance.

Nevertheless, Marsden concentrated agriculturally on his black-faced Suffolk sheep, a briskly maturing breed, which produced a quicker return of meat for the local market and which had been shipped to Australia on the convict ships. But he took his Merinos to New

Zealand and introduced a new industry there: in a part of the world that had never previously seen cows or horses or, indeed, sheep.

Antipodean history now mostly remembers him as a despised priest – except in New Zealand where, not having been a magistrate, his reputation has a much gentler texture and he is recognised mainly as the man who converted Maoris to Christianity.

Captain Macarthur continued to develop his industry by crossbreeding his Merinos with different stock while sourcing other Merinos to produce a pedigree flock. He travelled widely, trusting the development of the sheep in his absence to his wife Elizabeth and particularly to his flock-master, Edward Thoroughgood, in creating both cross-breed and pure Merino wool for export. Never was a shepherd so appropriately named: the Merino flock was 4,000 strong even before Macarthur had been sent back to England.

Thus it was he, Macarthur, who would become acknowledged as 'the Father of the Australian Wool Industry'. The centenary of his death (1834) was commemorated with a postage stamp and in 1966 his portrait appeared on the issue of an Australian two-dollar banknote.

Macarthur's first exported Merino shipment – about 16,000lbs – arrived in 1813, by which time England's weavers had had the chance to appreciate its value. It was sold for more than £8,000, or about 120d per pound weight – nearly three times what Samuel Marsden's consignment had achieved. (The figures are imprecise because the wool would have been sold to weavers or middlemen in separate bales at auction.) They well out-bid the buyers from Rawdon.

The colony's most important export industry had begun. By the 1870s the Australian Wool Exchange would be trading 100,000 lbs of raw wool in a single afternoon.

Prices must have varied greatly because the records left by John Gaunt – father of Reuben Gaunt who would later employ 500 people in his Farsley and Pudsey mills – was buying 'Botany' (possibly cross-bred) wool at one shilling and seven-pence-halfpenny per pound in 1841.

Mills in Farsley had been sourcing their English wool from merchants in Leeds and, less frequently, Bradford. They could also buy Scottish wool at Skipton or Halifax, towns on, or close to, a traditional Scottish drove road. But the continuing influx of Marino meant that Australian wool shipped to Liverpool could be bought there and brought to Bradford and Leeds along the canal.

At Benjamin Gott's Armley mill, barges filled with

sacks of Australian Merino would moor alongside his newly named Botany Quay.

The introduction of Merino wool to Yorkshire changed the face, not only of Australia but also of the West Riding as a quality wool–making entity. Suddenly (in historic terms) it would compete with, and outstrip, the superior textile products of the rest of England, and of the rest of the world.

And 40 years after Macarthur's first shipment, more than 127 million lbs of 'Foreign and Commonwealth' wool was being imported. Working men could now wear finer and better–finished cloth than English gentry had worn half a century earlier.

Some could even dress like a king.

In 1934 the Hainsworth family – whose ancestors had turned down the first consignment of Samuel Marsden's Merino wool, generously and sportingly laid out and opened a memorial garden in his name on Farsley Town Street to honour the local man who had brought such prosperity to the district. The garden is on the actual site of the warehouse where the first barrel of Merino wool had been examined and rejected. But beyond that small monument, Marsden's name and his contribution to the industry has probably been forgotten in the northern hemisphere.

The 'Merino' wool had, in effect, gone half-way round the world and back again. The most important element in its development had actually been English. The earliest histories show that, for centuries, the best English wool had been considered superior to the

Spanish – they were the only recognised wool–growing nations in the world at that time – on account of its greater length and fineness.

Flanders' weavers mixed the two sources, but for high quality textiles they used only English; even the Spanish used English wool for their finest manufacture. Henry II (1154-89) decreed that any cloth made by a mixture of the two in England should be burnt.

English long–haired sheep

The Spanish improved their product by not only buying English fleeces, but also buying long and fine-haired English sheep and crossing them with their own, originally Moorish, Merinos and thereby creating the finest breed known to man.

Having taken so much trouble to create it, it is no small wonder that, for many years, the export of live Merinos from Spain had been a capital offence.

The Merino

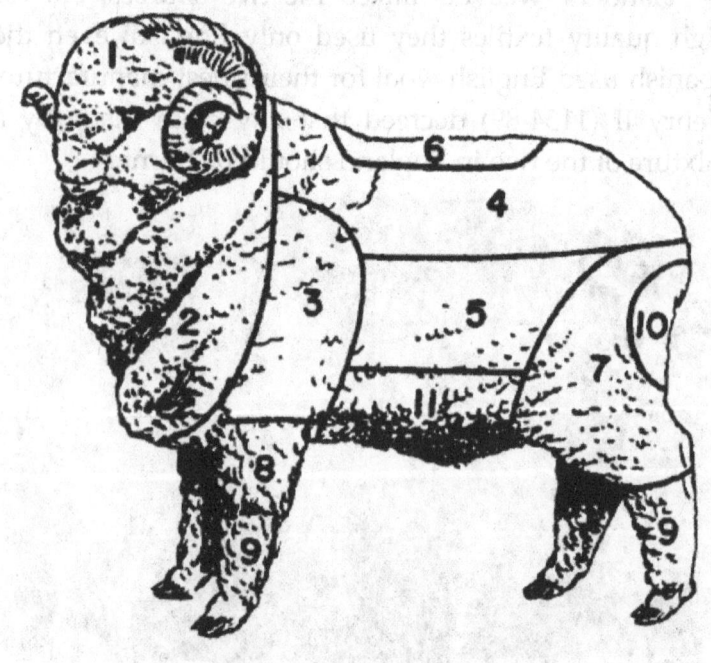

A (Merino) sheep and its different grades of fibre.:
1– Topknot; 2– Neck; 3– Shoulder; 4– Fleece; 5– Side; 6– Back; 7– Breech; 8– Arm; 9– Shank; 10– Stain; 11– Belly– stain.

A Merino ewe typically produces about 13lb (6.5kg) a year, and a fully grown ram about three times that weight. It is graded from 'strong' (broad) wool, through 'medium', 'fine', 'superfine', to 'ultra– fine'. Ultra– fine wool is suitable for blending with other fibres such as silk and cashmere.

Counting Sheep

In the beginning. weaving was an occupation of last resort for most shepherding families: they barely had the time for it.

The (probably urbanised) mental picture may well be the perfect pastural scene of a life in the healthy open air: vast acres of moorland with, at its centre, a be-smocked shepherd with a crook in his hand and an attentive collie at his feet. What that image does not show is that husbanding sheep is a 24-hour, seven-day, and all-weather occupation. 'Spring' lambing may seem idyllic – except that it invariably involves complications with lambs misaligned inside the womb, and a ewe incapable of ejecting its progeny after a five-month gestation; twin births are common, but the two lambs cannot be guaranteed to survive. Amateur veterinary skills are essential for shepherds and their wives. Some ewes may reject their own off–spring which then need feeding by human hand. The new males of the flock need castrating, because two rams in a sector will fight for dominance, charging literally head–to–head with sickening skull–crushing thuds until one of them drops dead. The parent rams have to be moved away from the attraction of their newly–born daughters.

And all the time the shepherd – and hopefully his

dog or dogs – needs to be alert to predation of the new lambs, from eagles, from wild dogs and (until the early 1820s when there was still a legal bounty available in Yorkshire for their carcasses or their skins) from wolves.

In winter, sheep can usually find long grass and dig as deep as about a foot to feed beneath snow. But, being soft-nosed, they are unable to break through ice, so in bad weather a flock needs to be rounded up in the snow and freezing sleet and brought closer to home – again, hopefully with human and canine ears and eyes constantly strained, alert for starving predators.

Although moorland sheep tend not to stray far, first thing every morning, and last thing at night, they had to be counted. Counting sheep may help some people to sleep, but the shepherd had to stay awake as the sheep meandered around their home patch. And he had his own language and method for doing it.

In Wharfedale and Swaledale, one to ten was: *Yan, Tan, Tethera, Mether, Pip, Azer, Sezar, Akker, Conter, Dick*. Then 10-20 would be based on the same words with '*dick*' (ten) as a suffix – except that 15 was *Bumfit* and 20 was *Jigget*. The count was a vigesimal system (based on 20) and the shepherd would put a stone in his pocket representing each 20 of his flock that he counted, and start again at *Yan...Tan...*

Other areas – including Scotland and Wales, and the West Country, had similar systems, with the words for numbers varying, in most cases only slightly, and possibly were originally Saxon.

There are folk songs about it: in some cities you can hear performers who have never been closer to a sheep than when eating a vegan 'lamb chop', forcing the ancient numbers to rhyme – or trying to emulate Jake Thackray, a Leeds teacher, who sang about his great aunt, Molly Metcalf, who was sent out to mind sheep in the Dales at the age of seven and died in the fields when she was 28.

The benefit of this day-long, year-round, all weather occupation by the shepherd was that he would have sheep milk for producing cheese, and meat to eat and salt for his larder, plus a surplus to sell. The lamb was for roasting, the mutton for pies and stews, and the old mutton for dog food (although not for his own dogs which would never be allowed to eat meat of any kind). And the sheepskins were for warmth.

A shepherd's wife would be responsible for the children, from birth through education: for victualling and cooking, baking and cleaning, and milking the ewes and cheese-making, along with responsibilities for the chickens and the egg production, caring for the sick animals, maintaining a kitchen garden and growing herbs for use as medicines, and probably for feeding and cleaning out a sty containing a pig or two and milking maybe half a dozen cows. She would quite likely also sew and mend clothes, and probably knit.

After that, there was the business of the wool.

Just Wool

Sheep require shearing in order to survive the heat of summer, even in Yorkshire. Otherwise they would shed it naturally – but usually not enough of it to ensure comfort.

It might be assumed that the shepherd would estimate how much wool was necessary to clothe his own family for the coming year. Then, when time was found for it, would be hands to the distaff (for spinning: which was usually the women's work) and to the loom (for weaving: a job done by men) for precisely that purpose. Even before shearing, there would have been sheep wool to pick from among thistle or gorse or along edges, or just shed onto the tough grass. They may also, if they found time, have done a bit more weaving to produce extra cloth, useful for bartering among their friends and neighbours, maybe if only because they would occasionally feel a preference for eating beef, instead of lamb, or need to buy a horse, or a wagon, or have a cartwheel mended, or a roof re-covered.

Theirs was mostly a cash-less society, offering little more than subsistence.

Once a year shepherds would steer their flock into the nearest stream for washing, wait for them to dry in the fresh air and then shear them and stack the wool, which they could trade. Eventually, travelling shearers – specialists at the job – would be employed, freeing the shepherds from an exhausting and exacting task.

Shearers would hope to handle every farm in one locality at the same time. They could be shearing thousands of sheep within a single period of a few days, often taking some of the better fleeces away with them.

In the interim period, between the departure of the shearers and the arrival of the wool-buyers, or the trip with it to market, the women and children would have washed the fleeces to prepare them for sale.

Wool, when carefully shorn from a sheep's back, produces 'a fleece' that – because strands of wool tend to cling together – looks like the single coat of the sheep from which it was trimmed (like a sheepskin rug, although without the leather backing). The shepherd's family would lay them out on the ground and pull off the skirts of dirty, dry, unkempt and matted rough edges.

One useful and important element in the creation of good wool was the abundance of soft, clean water for the necessary processes of its treatment: from the preparation of a sheep for shearing, for the cleansing of the fleece, and for degreasing. It would take time for the wool trade to realise the benefit of harnessing the energy of the fast-flowing water as a source of power, but what mattered was the softness, the lack of lime in the water that naturally enhanced the fineness and softness of even the coarsest wool.

Washed, each fleece would be laid out in the fresh air, perhaps draped over a stone wall or a slatted table, to dry. While there it would be beaten or 'broken' with a willow branch to help loosen any remaining foreign matter. But it would still not be clean enough to be presented for sale, and certainly not clean enough for spinning: there were still likely to be clinging insects, bits of vegetation, maybe even faeces, present in the wool and these all needed to be teased out of the fibres. Originally the spiny flower head of a teasel (*dipsacus*) plant would be used for this careful stroking and cleansing of the strands (the name comes from the Old English 'tease' meaning to separate or divide; the word 'thistle' comes from the same linguistic root).

Only after this process was raw wool acceptable to the buyers. For some sheep-herding families, while probably setting aside sufficient wool for their own needs, this was as far as the wool process went.

Itinerate merchants or wool–pedlars would not be far behind the sheep shearers and could relieve a shepherd of his entire stock, at a mutually agreeable price. Provided only that he could get more for the sale of each fleece than he had paid for the shearing of it, it would mean a profit; it saved him the bother of storing and trying to sell his clip piece-meal, or of weaving it and going to market to sell his pieces. Otherwise the buyer would load a pack-horse with bales ('woolpacks') and would later sort them and grade them himself and get a higher price for the better–quality wool in market towns.

Where he found large quantities of clean re–sellable fleeces the buyer might make an exclusive deal to buy the entire clip from a farmer for several years ahead.

The canny shepherd, realising that his fleeces had a value, might, as an alternative, transport his fleeces to the nearest market town. Annual 'wool fairs' became a rare excuse for festivity in many parts of Yorkshire.

The cottage families could – if they had the time, and the energy and the inclination – spin the fibres of their fleeces into hanks of wool, thereby commanding a higher price; they could weave the yarn and sell their 'pieces' at market. Or they could merely clean the raw fleeces and sell them: far easier and quicker, and an immediate return.

The travelling pedlars, whose pack horses stamped out the footpaths and bridleways between villages and across the moors, would become known as 'staplers', presumably because they offered a staple price for the wool.

By the mid-1300s there were about 50 identifiably different grades of wool.

Yorkshire wool, from the moors and from the monasteries, may have been lacking in quality but it had the advantage of being available in quantity.

Wool from Lincolnshire and Herefordshire was longer and finer and far more highly rated. The very best Yorkshire sheep's outer wool was also long and fine, making it strong and easy to spin, while the inside fibres were soft and dense, providing insulation against the cold – and even against the heat.

Sadly, most of the Yorkshire sheep did not produce 'the best'. It was, however (and still is), generally ideal for making carpets, blankets, heavy coats, tweeds, cloaks and uniforms, rather than fine coats for the gentry. It was the merchants, not the isolated shepherds, who learnt of the comparative qualities of the wool they were trading.

These, middlemen, the buyers and judges of wool quality, could sort it firstly by eye – whether it was fine or course, whether it was stained or cleaned, whether the fibres were long or short, and so on. There could be ten different qualities of wool within a single fleece. And once armed with that basic knowledge the travelling dealer would know when he was selling the best, having bought at the cheapest price.

Meanwhile the shepherd – living on a few pence a week and making more from his mutton than from his wool – had no way of knowing whether his product was comparatively good or merely mediocre.

Or whether he had simply been 'fleeced'.

A King's Ransom

In the annals of the country, what is probably the first recorded mention of English weaving, and exporting, was in the eighth century, when the weavers of Mercia – a kingdom centred on the Trent valley that dominated England for three centuries from its capital in Tamworth – were making cloaks for Charlemagne's Europe. The weavers had cut corners (and cut their cloth) to the extent that in 796 the Holy Roman Emperor wrote to Mercia's King Offa, asking him to ensure that future exports would be 'made of the same pattern that used to come to us in olden time'.

For several centuries 'raw' wool – wool straight off the sheep's back, neither spun nor woven – was the most valuable commodity in England, second only to cash or ready money, and far more plentiful.

In 1194, when Henry VI, a later Holy Roman Emperor, demanded ransom of 150,000 marks (100,000 pounds of silver, or about £30million today) for England's King Richard I, the amount was paid almost entirely in raw wool – a year's supply, 'borrowed' from the Cistercian monasteries, including all 200 estates of Fountains Abbey and those of Rievaulx, Kirkstall and Roche, near Maltby.

[The mark, introduced to England by the Danes,

was a currency, but never a coin. Its value was 13 shillings and fourpence – two-thirds of 'one pound sterling', which was the value of a pound of silver.]

Although schoolchildren – or, more likely, followers of the Robin Hood fables – are probably aware that the Lionheart was held to ransom, and maybe even that rich monasteries were relieved of their gold plate, English history teaching does not normally include the price demanded for his freedom. Nor, importantly, how it was paid. (Some 'church plate' was indeed collected, but was returned by Richard's mother, Queen Eleanor, as being unnecessary to secure her son's release.)

The ransom seems, however, to have been the first time that 'wool' (as the raw product of cloth) would be mentioned in any history of England. To be pedantic, it was the first mention of wool recounted in the first complete history of England (written by a Frenchman and published in 1724). And perhaps the first time that its value had been so vividly appropriated.

In a similar vein, it is probably well known that in the House of Lords the Lord Chancellor and the judges sit on woolsacks – precisely in order to show the importance of that product to the English economy and history. What remains unknown is when this tradition actually started (it was most likely during the reign of Edward III, but nobody knows for certain). Nor, probably, is it known that when the 'woolsacks' were opened in 1938 they were found to be stuffed with horsehair and at that stage were repacked with hanks of wool from different parts of the Commonwealth – again to emphasise the importance of wool to the economy. It seems reasonable to guess that none of this is the stuff of school history lessons.

Perhaps sadly, the shepherd, isolated on the moor or in the monasteries (or both) would also have been unaware of the true worth of his produce.

Once they had clothed themselves the family (and the monks) could set about the business of selling wool in its raw state, without necessarily knowing that they were feeding the insatiable looms of the Low Countries, Italy, Germany, France and Spain, where there was quality weaving but insufficient good wool.

But weaving it was a local and national necessity – people needed clothes. And the canny shepherd doubtless saw, when going to market, the mark-up between the cost of imported textiles and the price he had been paid for his wool.

It is easy to surmise that, within a single family unit there might be more sons and daughters than were essential for the running of either the flock or the household. The answer, for some – if not for all – was to spin their own yarn and weave, and maybe even to tailor, their own cloth pieces.

Spinning a Yarn

Until the invention of the spinning wheel, the practice of turning fleeces into yarn for weaving had not changed since Old Testament times when – according to the Book of *Proverbs*, (linked with Solomon, 971-931BC) 'the virtuous woman' –

> 'seeketh wool, and flax, and worketh willingly with her hands... She layeth her hands to the spindle, and her hands hold the distaff.'

Pearson Scott Foresman.

While *Exodus* noted that

> All the women that were wise hearted did spin with their hands, and brought that which they had spun, both of blue, and of purple, and of scarlet, and of fine linen.

We know little as fact of the old country traditions of domestic spinning. But it is asserted (by stories passed down the generations) that girls would carry their wool and their distaff – wrapping the fibres around a pole that was held in the crook of one arm, and then pulling the fibres from it and twisting them together around the spindle (and eventually their small spinning wheels) – to a different house each night; they would sit sharing the local gossip while carding and spinning, story–telling and singing.

It is also said that, weather permitting, Yorkshire women would take their spinning out onto the village green.

Until at least the 13th century, the economic factor in the wool trade had been just that – the trade in wool.

Those people who could spin would turn the fleece into yarn for those who – most likely on their home-made looms, copying the style of the Romans – would weave it, and those who could, would cut and tailor the fabric into clothing.

But it was hardly an industry.

It was easiest to do what everybody else was doing everywhere in England: just growing wool on the sheep's back. And selling it.

The King's Tax On Sacks

A significant but maybe small and necessary amount of native English wool was kept at home. Sales at Yorkshire's wool fairs attracted buyers from Hull, Pontefract, York, Lincoln and Newcastle upon Tyne, but the great majority of wool went to foreign merchants. In one instance (around 1290) an Italian buyer bought the entire output from Kirkstall Abbey's sheep for ten years into the future.

Not all trade was for cash. A tract published in 1436 would record that some Venetian buyers brought with them rhubarb to exchange for wool – perhaps thereby sparking what would become another Yorkshire speciality – along with senna, scammony and similar 'licking stuff'. It might appear that the English diet of the period created plenty of digestive complications.

The problem was that the regular weavers had insufficient raw wool to keep their looms busy.

So much wool was exported that English tailors complained about the shortage of cloth.

Twice in the mid-1200s the export of raw wool was banned, suggesting that there was an insufficiency for the clothing industry, and also creating evidence of a deprived tailoring lobby with sufficient clout to gain royal attention. [The fraternity of tailors would eventually become the Merchant Tailors' Guild.]

Having failed to stop it, in 1275 Edward I had the bright idea that it would be a good and easy solution to put a tax on it at the ports: it would pay for his military adventurism against Scotland, Wales and France.

Wool was weighed by the *tod*, which was usually measured at 28lb. The standard sack of wool for export was 364 pounds in weight, and it was calculated that approximately 240 sheep were needed to provide the wool required for one sack.

In 1280 about 27,000 (taxed) sacks of wool were exported from England. Wool was light, and its value-to-weight ratio was high; it was therefore an ideal product for shipping.

The Florentines were well represented in England that year, not only touring the Yorkshire monasteries and sourcing the best wool to send home to their new booming weaving and tailoring industries, but (perhaps equally interestingly) also as revenue collectors for the Pope.

The Vatican had experienced difficulty in extracting taxes from the English monasteries, probably because monks didn't deal much with money. So the Frescobaldi family, already trading with the monasteries, offered its services and took on the role of Papal merchant bankers. (A local rival Florentine family, the Medici, were the regular Papal bankers.)

Their method of tax collection was simple: since the monks had no money the Frescobaldi traders took wool instead. They sent it back home to Florence where weavers were paying the highest prices for the best wool. It was an all-round success: the monks paid with wool, not money, the Frescobaldi got the best wool in England (the absolute best from 49 of the 74 Cistercian monasteries, and usable quality from the rest), buying at the lowest price for converting into fine textiles saleable at high values... and the Vatican received its due taxes in cash at the base value of the wool.

Not surprisingly, this greatly impressed the English exchequer which was trying to squeeze money out of wool-spinning priests and peasants, who didn't have much, and big landowners who seemed always to find ways to avoid paying any. And most importantly from exporters who were sailing away without having paid duty on their wool. In 1277 the Frescobaldi family had loaned the English king money to finance his castle building in Wales and by the end of the century – one loan having led to another – had become chief bankers to the crown, as well as to the Vatican. But Edward, in a near constant state of war, had no way of paying his debts directly so in 1300 the family was given control of the exchanges (meaning all coinage transactions) in London, Canterbury, Newcastle upon Tyne, Hull, Bristol, Exeter and Dublin.

And because his officers had found little success in collecting taxes from exported wool, in 1306 Edward gave the Frescobaldi family control of the customs houses in virtually every major English port.

The Frescobaldi loaned the king more money to finance his wars, but now they were getting repayment by way of the customs duties on wool that were being paid directly to them, rather than to the exchequer.

Most of the Frescobaldi family left the comparative comfort, sophistication and deference to which they had been accustomed in their palaces (they owned several) in Florence.

One of the Frescobaldi, Giovanni, wrote a letter to other family members who were coming to join him about how to deal with the English:

> Do not wear bright colours.
> Look as though you are stupid, but make sure you stay on your toes.
> Give the appearance of being generous.
> Pay your way as you go.
> When you collect your debts do it courteously, suggesting that you are the poor one.
> Do not get too nosey.
> Buy whenever you see a bargain, but be wary of deals that involve men of the court.
> Do as you are told by those who hold the power, and make sure you stay on good terms with your fellow Italians.
> Lock and bolt your door early at night.

In 1307 Edward II inherited the throne and, with it, his father's debts and the concessions he had made to the Florentines.

By the end of 1305, the number of taxed sacks exported annually had been no more than 32,300. Between 1305 and 1310 the number of sacks of raw wool that were taxed on export averaged more than 39,000 a year – the product of around one million sheep – the highest number it had ever been. Nevertheless, the income collected from taxes was not keeping pace with the rates of borrowing.

In 1311, when a nobleman could live comfortably

on £20 a year, the Crown's unpaid loans from the Frescobaldi family amounted to more than £155,000. Their new importance, acknowledged by the appointment of Berto Frescobaldi as a Privy Counsellor in 1310, infuriated the native feudal barons who claimed that the foreigners had too much control over the crown.

The following year the Florentines were driven out of the country and their assets, so to speak, were confiscated (that is, they were written off).

Relieved of their commissions and dues, they returned home to their textile industry, only to be faced with an anti–establishment guild of textile craftsmen organised by the rival Medici family: they were no longer welcome there, either. So, with time on their hands they turned to a secondary agricultural product and created what has been described as the best Chianti in the world on their Tuscan estates.)

The Frescobaldi Chianti label features one of the family coats of arms with a sheepskin, reflecting their connection with the wool trade and industry.

Get Weaving

The Romans (in northern England for three centuries) had introduced the horizontal loom and had a wool–weaving centre in Winchester. They wore wool as tunics under their armour and for overcoats or cloaks and for underwear and socks. They discovered that it was warm in winter and virtually waterproof, and yet surprisingly cool (and sweat absorbing) in summer. They even used woven or knitted squares of wool as 'toilet paper'; it was soft to the skin and then washable and re-useable – an early (probably the first) example of the 'recycling' of any woollen product.

When the Normans came to England sheep were the dominant animal. Sheep breeds were not given names; they were simply classified by the type of wool produced in different parts of the country, which in turn was dictated by regional and nutritional variations in grazing.

Yorkshire's varied landscape produced both short, course hairs and (fewer) long, fine and strong ones.

Calverley is a hill village half–way between Leeds and Bradford; it includes the township of Farsley and has boundaries with Rawdon (north), Pudsey (south), Rodley and Bramley (east, on the Aire), and Thornbury (south-west, a suburb of Bradford) and now merges almost imperceptibly with all of them: a border milepost on the main road reads Bradford 5, Leeds 5.

Notably, in the 1250s at least five fulling mills were recorded within the parish. Fullers were the men who (sometimes using 'fullers' earth', a mild clay-based mixture, as a cleansing agent) washed the lanolin and other oils and any foreign matter out of the rough pieces that had been woven in the cottages, possibly for family use but in quantities that suggest it was also for sale.

The Old Testament has references to launderers' fields and washers' pools, which would be where raw woven cloth would be 'fulled' – removing animal oil, dirt and other impurities and pounding by fist, feet or wooden clubs to make wool thicker. Then the wool was whitened by soaking it in stale human urine, for its ammonia content – before being thoroughly rinsed in fresh and, ideally, fast–running, water.

Then they washed and pounded the finished pieces to shrink, stabilise and clean the cloth.

According to *Ezekiel* (27:18) Damascus was the source of the whitest wool.

In the *New Testament* the apostle *Mark* (9:3) reports that, after the transfiguration of Christ:

> His raiment became shining, exceeding white as snow; so as no fuller on earth can white them.

We know a bit more about Roman citizens, who wore the 'toga' – 40 to 60 square feet of broad white woollen cloth draped around the body and held in place at the waist by a cord. Both Pliny and Suetonius wrote about washing, whitening and thickening cloth.

Beating the woven fabric in a *fullonica* also matted the threads, which cling together like Velcro, making them stronger and the fabric more waterproof. According to Pliny, writing *Natural History* in 77AD, one advantage of the job was that:

> 'Men's urine relieves gout, as is shown by the testimony of fullers, who for that reason claim that they never suffer from the malady'.

Urine was in so much demand in ancient Rome that the emperor Vespasian, who ruled from 69 to 79AD, put a tax on it. French public urinals, to this day, are known as *vespasiennes*; in Italy, *vespasiani*.

Yorkshire clothiers (in this book a 'clothier' is anybody who works with 'cloth' or 'stuff') were still collecting and using 'stale' urine in the mid-1800s. They referred to it politely as 'old wash'.

The idea of weaving the raw wool instead of exporting it and then importing the textiles (sometimes in the form of ready–made clothing) had caught on in England. There were, after all, English tailors; there always had been. They may not have had the finesse of the continental counterparts, but people had to be clothed, somehow. The tailors needed woven cloth and the weavers of it – not all of them shepherds – needed spun wool. The spinners – not all of them shepherds' wives or daughters – needed fleeces. The staplers had a choice: namely to sell the wool to weavers or to go through the palaver of carting their sacks to the coast and trying to avoid the revenue collectors for a higher price, or to consider the simpler economics of moving the raw wool only from country to town. The wool-into-cloth trade soon became so important that professional guilds were inaugurated to control textile quality. They were established in Lincoln in 1131 and in London, Winchester, Nottingham, Huntingdon and Oxford, before York (1164).

In 1274 cloth makers in Whitby and Selby (North Riding) and in Hedon (East Riding) were accused of manufacturing cloth 'in dimensions contrary to the assize laid down in Magna Carta'.

It may surprise the reader (as it surprised this writer) to find that *Magna Carta*, which famously sets out the rights and freedoms of the English subjects of King John, should be concerned about the dimensions of textile pieces. But diligent research shows that it is there, in Clause 35 of the *Charter*:

> 'There shall be standard measures of wine, ale, and corn (the London quarter), throughout the kingdom. There shall also be a standard width of dyed cloth, russet, and haberject, namely two ells within the selvedges. Weights are to be standardised similarly.'

Magna Carta was the first legal effort to regularise weights and measures to facilitate trade.

Oddly, the *Charter* did not specify a minimum length for a piece of cloth: oddly, because, for centuries one of the problems would be of cloth merchants selling short.

The 'standard' length of a piece of cloth could, and would, vary – from 12 yards (a 'Northern Dozen') to 60, but they did not always match their description. A bit like King Offa's cloaks.

While it is evident that the 'manufacturing' industry had a presence in the West Riding, it was clearly nowhere close to being a monopoly – not even within the county. There was competition from weavers from Teesside to the river Don. And while the textiles of York and Beverley were rated alongside the finest from Norfolk, Lincoln, Stamford and elsewhere – for which arose a big demand from abroad – the rural cloths were of inferior quality and coarse texture, and were not even rated on the home market. The difference was reflected in the price: while a bolt of Beverley Blue might command six shillings a yard, the poorest West Riding weaver might be lucky if his cloth sold at six pence (a twelvefold differential).

Nevertheless, the Yorkshire weavers could, if they worked at it, satisfy some of the needs of the county's wealthy and all the needs of the poor. There were plenty of happy rural amateurs who were prepared, when otherwise unemployed, to attend to casual work on the loom. Others were content with the simpler industry of providing 'raw' wool that was saleable for home consumption or for export.

But there were to be many long years of selling raw wool before the West Riding – centred on Bradford – would become known as the world capital for weaving cloth, and before Leeds became the centre for trading it (and for trading just about anything else).

In the archives of the county, Whitby was recorded as a wool weaving town, long before Bradford would produce its first piece of worsted.

Weavers in York and Beverley led the way by showing that there could be a profit in weaving the wool instead of selling it in its raw state, and the two great religious centres, saving the longest and finest fibres for their own worsteds, competed in quality, while also vying for control of the merchandising of their products.

The distinction of being the first West Riding clothier in documented history of the industry may belong to one Alexander Fuller of Leeds who, in 1275, was fined for making cloth that was 'not of the legal width'. (No mention in the indictment of *Magna Carta*.)

There was, however, early evidence of surnames that suggest some strong connections with the industry: at Leeds in 1201, Simon the Dyer was fined for selling wine 'contrary to the legal assize', clearly indicating that he was involved in trades other than dyeing; Robertus Tynctor de Ledes (a tinctor also being a dyer) was named in a Kirkstall Abbey charter in the late 1230s; and documents from 1258 record the names of William Webster (weaver), and John Lister (tinctor), and Richard and Andrew Taillur, (from the Latin *taliare*: to cut). The surnames Weaver and Walker (fuller) became much more commonplace and Merchant (or Marchant), Chapman and Mercer – all of them meaning trader – also started to appear in the records of Leeds.

And it is therefore clear that, while most of the country was obsessed with the idea of selling its raw wool, in Yorkshire a lot of people were weaving it.

The use of the term 'wool industry' can be confusing. The industry was actually divided into two main parts, woollens and worsteds. The distinction depended on the type of wool used. During the 18th century

Yorkshire developed as the country's major centre for woollen production while there was much later a surge in development of the worsted industry around (but not actually in) Bradford.

Prior to the 18th century worsted production had been concentrated in East Anglia.

Worsted (named after the Norfolk village of Worstead) refers to both the yarn and the cloth woven from it, produced by a technique taught (in Norfolk) by Flemish émigré weavers using long–strand pasture wool that was combed into parallel lines, then tightly twisted in the spinning process. Yorkshiremen – already using the same system – would later say that that wool spun in this way had been 'wusted', using the placename as a verb. It produced finer, smoother, lighter and cooler material than woollen fabric. Worsted cloth has a natural 'recovery', meaning that it is resilient and quickly returns to its original shape. It is the perfect material for making tailored suits, while 'woollen', made from the shorter fibres scrunched loosely together, was ideal for warm sweaters and blankets and overcoats and in its spun form, in hanks for knitting.

There were therefore two wool weaving industries: the worsted cloth industry and the woollen industry. Both involved working up sheep's wool; however they were using different raw materials (sometimes from the same animal) that required different techniques of production. Worsteds are made of long wool fibres and woollen cloths are made of short wool fibres.

These different fibres need a special preparation in order to be spun; there are different processes of spinning, and the cloths are finished differently.

Since most of the natural sheep grease (lanolin) had been lost in the washing, the wool needed to be re-greased lightly with a vegetable oil or with butter (sometimes with goose grease) to make it more easily workable. Some homeworkers tried to skip this step by washing the wool less vigorously, and leaving some of the lanolin in the fibre.

Then it would be sorted again according to thickness and length so that similar strands could be attached to each other.

Next came the carding and the long fine hairs were sorted from the shorter, thicker, ones. Then the wool from the card was rolled into a cigar shape and was – finally – ready for spinning. Carding was a job usually done by the children in a family home, preparing for spinning yarn into woollens. Combing was a further process, producing lines of fibre that would create cleaner, finer and stronger yarn for spinning into worsteds. Each individual wool fibre has an outer layer of microscopic scales or barbs. When two hairs come in contact these scales tend to cling and stick to each other. It is this physical clinging and sticking that allows wool fibres to be spun into thread so easily by simply connecting and lightly twisting.

Those were the skill-sets: the scouring, spinning and the weaving, passed down through generations, with children at their parents' sides watching, learning and gradually assisting with the processes.

From the early Middle Ages – the time of the Crusades – and well into the 1800s, weaving woollen cloth was a totally cottage industry: sheep's wool was carded or combed and spun to make fibre for weaving on a hand loom.

But a family might have a few dozen, or many hundred, sheep, grazing on common moorland or in farms rented from the lord of the local manor or the local monastery, all being sheared at the same time each year. There would be a surplus – often a vast one – in the number of fleeces produced.

That was fortunate – because there was always a ready market for the raw wool. And for many centuries, in Yorkshire and beyond, that would remain as the dominant trade: the simple production of raw wool, far more than the industrious weaving of it.

Fulling was one of the final stages of the cloth-making process: beating the cloth in water caused it to shrink in both length and width, but its density made it resistant to both wear and weather. Woven properly, the fibres would be so closely matted that the pattern of weaving was scarcely visible.

England's first fulling mill was built by the Knights Templar at Temple Newsam (Leeds) in 1185, but the existence of so many fullers in one small community like Calverley suggests that a great number of pieces that came to them were ready for the family or for the market – although there would be no mention of any actual weaving in the area for another hundred years.

Obviously, however, somebody living locally was producing a sufficient amount of cloth to keep five mills in employment fulling it. This was clearly cloth being woven for a ready market.

A survey covering the Manor Mill at Baildon in 1285 refers to *two mills, one for corn, the other a fulling mill*. A water wheel in the River Aire lifted and dropped heavy wooden hammers onto pieces of cloth in a tank below water level, matting (thickening) and cleansing them. At the time of the survey the population of the village cannot have been much more than 30 – yet there was a sufficient home production of wool to require a mechanical fulling process.

But communication was scant: and so were records. As far as is known, in the rest of the West Riding, people were still stamping on their cloth.

Considering that the primary occupation of most rural people was near-subsistence farming – keeping a couple of cows and a few pigs and hens, in addition to their sheep roaming at will on local moorland – and that weavers were their own masters, working only when it suited them, there was clearly an awful lot of weaving going on.

It seems likely that the fullers had organised a mill, or some sort of milling activity, on the banks of the Aire or of one of the fast-flowing streams that fed it. Actual fulling mills (dedicated buildings) had started to appear all over the Riding even before the introduction of an Act in 1376 requiring that all cloths had to be properly fulled before export – the first official recognition that wool was being woven and exported.

In 1277 William the Fuller and Ralph de Wortley were paying two pounds a year to rent a mill at Wakefield, which, to judge only from its price, must have been handling a lot of woven pieces before the cutting-up into garments by the cottage-dwellers or being placed on sale in the cloth booths of the weekly markets. (Wakefield also had its traders: in 1274 there were Philip the Mercer, William Chapman and Philip the Tailor, living alongside a number of other Merchants and Marchants).

In the Calder valley fulling mills were established at Sowerby, Halifax, Rastrick, Dewsbury, Mirfield and Ossett. But the business extended way beyond the narrow area that would become (and be remembered) as its centre.

In Skipton (previously *Shipton* = 'sheep town') there were Isabel Webster and Thomas Webster, both weavers (the Old English word *webbestre* originally meant a female weaver). In the Vale of York we find fullers at Pocklington, tailors and fullers at Thorp Arch; fullers and dyers at Aberford, Alwoodley, Aysgarth, Stokeseley and Pickering; and a flourishing trade at Northallerton, Ripon and Yarm. The dye-house at Richmond was rented for four pounds a year.

On manorial lands the fulling mills would be built by the landowner and leased out to entrepreneurial villagers, with tenants being instructed to use the manorial mill and no other. The Bradford fulling mill, for example, became a monopoly, leased for 10 shillings a year in the 1350s by two brothers appropriately called Walker (in Scotland fullers walked on the cloth to the tune of 'waulking songs'). The lease decreed that no other fuller could set up a business within the lands of the Lord of Bradford – nor could any local clothier take his pieces outside the area to be processed.

The number of locally archived references to fulling proves that the business of weaving pieces for that trade – even though it does not appear to be recorded as such – was considerable.

On Tenterhooks

After fulling, the woven piece might be dyed (to disguise any natural discolouration) using woad, from plant leaves, for blue, and also with madder and lichens for reds or purples. 'Stale urine', already in use as a whitener, was also – somehow – discovered to be a mordant (a fixer) for the dyes.

But it was most often left as white, so that buyers could choose their own colour, then it was hung out to dry in the open air on sloped wooden frames known as 'tenters' (Latin: *tent* = stretched), and fastened against the wind by 'tenterhooks' which also helped the fabric to avoid shrinking too much, while not stretching it far enough to thin or weaken it.

In Yorkshire winters, tentering was taken indoors to a room that was heated by a fireplace.

Cloth left out to dry in the night air was at risk of being stolen. In Halifax, because wool was so precious a commodity, theft of cloth became a capital offence. In fact until 1650 the penalty for stealing any item worth 14 pence or more could lead to beheading on the gibbet (an instrument similar to the guillotine). Apparently there was another gibbet at Hull, also prescribed for minor crimes, hence the *Beggar's Prayer*, written by John Taylor in 1639:

> At Halifax, the law so sharp doth deal,
> That whoso more than 13 pence doth steal;
> They have a gyn that wondrous, quick and well,
> Sends thieves all headless unto Heaven or Hell.
> From Hell each man says Lord, deliver me,
> Because from Hell can no redemption be.
> Men may escape from Hull and Halifax,
> But sure in Hell, there is not heavier tax.
> Let each one for themselves in this agree,
> And pray – from Hull, Hell and Halifax
> Good Lord, deliver me.

Woven pieces could be sold at the tented stage in the process – or before dyeing, so that the end-user could arrange them to suit his intended market. But it was still considered to be 'unfinished'.

In its still raw woven form the cloth would often appear to be rough and possibly hairy, with stray wool fibres, especially if made from crimped or curly woollen yarn. The fuzzy surface was teased up from the cloth, creating a nap which would then be cropped off to provide a smooth finish.

The croppers (sometimes also known as 'shearers') used large hand shears, about four feet long and weighing more than 40lbs (18kg) that had changed little since the time of the Romans. They dragged one blade down the cloth and cropped any protrusions with the other blade.

Cropping could make or break a piece of cloth, so it was seen as a specialist trade – not one to be done casually at home in bad light by spinners or weavers – and most cropping was done in small independent buildings that were set up all around the district and became known as 'cropping shops'.

Cloth-shearer: George Walker

The croppers developed a large callus (called a saddle) on their forearm after using the shears for several years, and it was said at the time that 'you could tell a cropper by his saddle'.

Having been made smooth, the fabric would need to be 'teased' (using the head of the teasel plant) again to restore a minimum amount of fine napping. Too much, and the shearing had to be done again: just right and the textile felt, between finger and thumb, to be fine wool, as intended. The amount of teaseling and shearing that was applied determined the quality and end-use of each piece of cloth. It was the most highly rated skill in the entire process.

Even then, for the finest quality of fabric there was a final appraisal to be made. The diligent weaver or, most likely, the merchant who had opted to do the 'finishing' himself, would check the piece, inch by inch, inspecting for flaws. These might be 'burls' (knots) or 'slubs' (extra thicknesses) in the yarn; sometimes a line of weft thread might have been missed. These flaws – while being possibly unnoticeable to the unskilled eye – needed to be resolved and painstakingly replaced, invisibly, and by hand. This process was known as 'burling and mending' or burling and finishing. In time, small factories staffed by skilled and patient women would be set up, to do nothing else.

And, once improved, the piece that had been spun from the washed and combed fleece, woven, fulled, tented, dyed, dried, sheared, teaselled and inspected and perfected would be folded into squares, pressed in a wooden vice and presented for sale: smooth, soft and luxurious, fit for the finest clothing.

Every single stage in the process was another opportunity for perfection. And perfection throughout was what produced perfect cloth, with the highest financial return, and which would eventually lead to skills and individual craftsmanship.

… Or, they could just sell their wool in its raw state.

Edward, Wool King

In 1337 Edward I's grandson, Edward III, looked for more and higher taxes to support the great expense of his army in what was to be called the Hundred Years War (it lasted 116 years, ending in 1453) and one pretext would be that the war was being fought by England to protect Flanders, its important trading partner, from invasion by the French. (The English King had married a Flemish princess, Philippa of Hainault, who became his 'political advisor' and acted as Regent when the king was abroad, fighting in the war.)

Exports of raw wool had fallen – not only because access to French ports was closed, but because many Flemish weavers, fullers, dyers and merchants, fearing the threat of war and of coming under French control, had fled from Ypres, Brabant, Malines, Ghent, Bruges and Louvain and moved to England, a nearby and friendly nation. They settled in places they knew of from the wool trade, quite a few of them in York, and some in Halifax, but also in Norfolk and Suffolk, in the West Country, the Cotswolds, Cumberland and the Yorkshire Dales.

So with an increase in experts and a decline in exports and a surplus of wool on hand, there was an obvious solution: if the Belgians, the Germans and the

Italians could do it, so could the English. From a nation of wool producers they became a nation of weavers. Instead of shipping the raw wool they would get weaving with it.

During Edward III's reign there were cloth makers as well as tailors and drapers in Leeds, but Pontefract was actually the biggest town in the Riding at the time; Leeds was only ninth, numerically – in fact smaller in population than Selby, Tickhill, Rotherham and Snaith.

But while the tax – when it was collected – was useful, there was insufficient home produce to feed the looms to make the fabric for tailors to clothe the nation. An increase in taxation, intended to stop, or at least to reduce, the profits of raw wool exports and to keep English wool for English looms seemed to present more of a challenge than a hindrance for the illegal shippers.

The record of government Acts during Edward's reign suggests that weaving was a subject that did not concern most of the population – including shepherds and the wool merchants – as much as it bothered him. It also exposed the King's dilemma: he wanted his tax paid on the export of wool, but he did not want the country's wealth to be expended on importing its foreign return as cloth or clothing.

In 1331 the King granted his protection to John Kempe, a Flemish weaver, who came to exercise and to teach his skills, and he offered the same deal to fullers and dyers and other related trades who wished to leave the war zone and settle in England.

In 1336 the same conditions were offered to two weavers from Brabant in the south Netherlands who settled in York. A year later another pair of weavers would arrive in the city, followed by 15 weavers from Zealand.

These foreigners by no means introduced weaving to Yorkshire (and the rest of the country) – as we have already seen, it had been sufficiently important to have been mentioned in Magna Carta, 100 years earlier – but they certainly showed the way in terms of industry and more especially of quality.

English weaving expanded under their influence, to the extent that a new Act decreed that no (raw) wool should be exported out of the realm by any local or foreign merchant upon pain of death (an Act that was repealed shortly afterwards). And further, that no more cloths or clothing could be imported; even the wearing of foreign cloth (coats, dresses, trousers or caps) was prohibited.

Later, the king promised his protection to all clothworkers from foreign lands who wanted to dwell and work in England with sufficient freedom to carry on with their trades. The immigrants needed protection, because the natives originally saw them as rivals for business (perhaps also as more skilled competitors) and smashed their looms.

By some glitch in communication, Edward has been credited with 'inventing' the English clothing industry by 'importing' Flemish weavers, apparently overlooking the fact that they had voluntarily fled their homeland and arrived as political refugees. They were coming, whether they were invited or not.

Those few citizens of Leeds who are aware that the

Black Prince (another Edward) was Edward III's son and who assume that his bronze statue in City Square is there as a sign of respect and credit for the king who introduced foreigners to teach the town its most important industry are therefore similarly misguided.

It seems, in any case, an odd idea to show respect for a man by erecting a statue of his son. There is, however, an oblique connection with wool and the Black Prince. It was in the Battle of Crécy` – in which, in 1346 as then heir to the throne, he 'won his spurs' for chivalry. We were taught that at school. What we did not learn was that the war was largely fought to protect vital English trade routes for wool across continental Europe while defending Flanders, its important trading partner, against threats from the French.

But in fact the statue, which was unveiled in 1903 to commemorate Leeds' city status ten years earlier, has no connection whatsoever with either the city or its industry.

In other words, people from the Low Countries, whether they were weavers or not, had a presence since the Battle of Hastings, and the record of Yorkshire surnames proves that the varying arts of weaving were being practiced long before the king's intervention.

This does not, however, detract from the influence that Edward III had on the textile industry.

Prior to his reign the production of wool had been virtually a free-for-all and Edward attempted, with a large degree of success, to bring some sense and sensibility into it, and to protect the English weavers by reducing the import of foreign textiles.

However, Edward's reign was also marked by a series of Scottish raids (which penetrated as far south as the West Riding), by agricultural famine, and by the Black Death (1348-49), a plague that carried away an estimated half of the entire population of Yorkshire.

Perhaps it was unfortunate that the Flemish clothiers did not bring more of their experience to the West Riding, for while York and Beverley would continue to flourish and produce cloth of quality, and even to improve it, until the end of the 18th century the products of the Aire and Calder would continue to be considered as being of an inferior grade. Even in the 17th century, when Yorkshire weavers were using the same wool as their counterparts in the West Country, their finished cloths were rated as no more than average.

Edward's overall plan was nevertheless successful. The manufacture of woollen textiles began to expand in the villages, and towns and England would suddenly be exporting more (untaxed) cloth pieces than raw wool.

This necessitated a life changing experience for families – from merely shepherding and shearing to becoming the creators of saleable textiles on even a small domestic scale. The source of woollen yarn and cloth had mostly been the province of self-employed families – even, perhaps, of 'happy' families – because they had always worked at a speed and at a rate and at times that suited them, and they worked from home, attending to the wool when they had nothing to do on the home farm that was more important to them.

Every shepherds' cottage had the wherewithal to

make sufficient cloth for a family's clothing; or maybe a few friendly villagers had access to a loom that they could share. The women would have picked out the strands of a fleece that they needed for a garment, cleaned them and aligned them for spinning, and then their men would weave the yarn into cloth. Just enough, perhaps, to make a jacket or coat. And when time was available to weave a piece of cloth for sale.

What was changing was the factor of scale.

At the start of the 100 Years War around 90 per cent of England's industry and economy had been the production of wool, mostly raw wool. Now it was changing into the production of processed wool, in the form of actual textiles. No longer a seasonal distraction following shearing time in early summer, sorting, spinning and weaving wool would become a year-round occupation.

Even though the quality of land in the West Riding was poor – good enough, in reality, only for raising sheep, agriculture was side-lined in favour of cloth-making.

The Riding's lack of distinction appears to have been the lack of any improvement in industrial skill along with a short supply of long-haired fleeces.

Norfolk, on the other hand, appeared to have both the right breed of sheep and the spinning and weaving know-how.

Because it hosted the biggest number of immigrant weavers, Norfolk became the main centre for textile production and marketing, and the parish of Worstead, 13 miles north of Norwich, still claims to have given its name as the origin of worsted cloth although as a style of weaving it had been practised in Yorkshire for years. What the immigrants may have done, with the local advantage of long-haired Norfolk sheep, was introduce a better quality of what they would call worsteds.

It may be of interest to note that, before the arrival of Edward III's immigrants, spinners and weavers in Yorkshire were making what they called 'worstede' or 'worset' – whenever they could find long-haired and fine-haired sheep.

Nevertheless, for centuries, the village of Worstead would be considered as the centre of 'worsted' trade – although whatever the Norfolk weavers learnt from the Flemish did not include reliable quality in weaving or honesty in trade.

According to an Act of 1467, there were –

> ...within the city of Norwich, as elsewhere within the county of Norfolk, divers persons who do make untrue wares of all manners of worsteds, not being of the assizes in length nor in breadth, not of good stuff and right making, as they ought to be, and of old time were accustomed... and yarn pertaining to them not well wrought, in great deceit...
>
> And whereas the worsteds in times past were lawfully wrought and merchandises well liked and greatly desired and esteemed in the parts beyond the sea, now because they be of no right making nor good stuff, they be reported and called subtle and unlawful merchandise, and of little reputation, to the great damage of our said lord the king, and great prejudice of his faithful people.

King's Wardens were appointed with full powers of search and arrest to check the quality of wool produced around the township of Worstead itself, and to bring any miscreants before a mayor or steward who would apply punishment 'at his discretion'. Mayoral discretion did not appear to be much of a deterrent, and Norfolk's reputation and manufacture would slowly diminish.

Very slowly. In fact from a reading of the multitude of early parliamentary Acts concerning wool it would be easy to get the impression that no place very far from the centre of Norfolk was involved in the wool trade in any way. Nor, at first, was it acknowledged to be. During the reign of Edward IV (1461-1483) worsted manufacture was extended across Norfolk, Suffolk and Cambridgeshire and in a minor way as far as Essex. Norfolk, however, remained its principal seat.

John Whitcomb, a wealthy manufacturer, employed 200 girls spinning wool in a single room:
> And in a chamber close beside
> Two hundred maidens did abide
> In petticoats of stammel red
> And milk white kerchers on their head.

It was the first description of factory girls, or mill girls as such. They would all have been spinning on the distaff. Norfolk had so much raw wool that it had to outsource some of it to Yorkshire spinsters, creating a virtual full-time job for women in a rival manufacturing county.

During the reign of Henry VIII (1509-1547) despite many attempts to promote its success by legislature, the Norfolk worsted industry was already in a state of decay.

Reformation

The popular image of Henry VIII may be one of richness and grandeur, but when he took the crown the monarchy was virtually bankrupt.

His break from the established Roman Church, along with his assumed position as head of the Church of England in 1533, brought him much needed wealth as, over four years, 800 monasteries were disbanded and their land and treasures taken for the Crown. Henry was now responsible for many thousands of sheep and the landlord of many sheep farms.

One early effect of the Reformation would be that Protestants from other countries – principally from the Netherlands, where the Catholic Inquisition had recently been introduced – fled in huge numbers to England to seek asylum and the freedom to practise their own form of religion without harassment, or worse. In that, they were mistaken. They arrived in an intensely Roman Catholic country that was naturally suspicious of foreigners – more so, when natives of the host country realised that many of the immigrants were weavers, who threatened their jobs.

Nowhere had this xenophobia a more rancorous root than in Yorkshire.

Dissent had started with a march, the 'Lincolnshire

Rising', involving 3,000 people angered by the dissolution of their abbey at Louth in October 1536.

With support from local gentry, a force estimated at 40,000 marched on Lincoln town and occupied their Cathedral. They demanded the freedom to continue worshipping as Roman Catholics and protection for the treasures of the Lincolnshire churches. But the rebels dispersed when the King's army confronted them.

The vicar of Louth and Nicholas Melton, a cobbler, were identified as the two main leaders of the rising and were both hanged at Tyburn.

Within a week the revolt had spread to Yorkshire where a London barrister called Robert Aske became the leader of many more people rebelling against the dissolution of their monasteries, calling themselves the 'Pilgrimage of Grace'.

Aske, from Aughton near Selby, led 9,000 people who occupied York, drove out the king's tenants from homes formerly used by monks, and took control of the Minster where Roman Catholic observances were resumed. Aske's revolt spread quickly to Cumberland, Northumberland and to north Lancashire, picking up people suffering from the previous year's poor harvest, high food prices and the loss of food and shelter that had been available to the poor from the monasteries.

In October the following year, the king promised the rebels a general pardon, a Parliament to be held at York within a year, and a reprieve for the abbeys until the parliament had met. Naively trusting the king's promises, Aske dismissed his followers.

More than 100 people were arrested, tried for

treason and sentenced to the traitors' death of being hanged, drawn and quartered: the king explaining that the so-called promise had been made falsely in his name. Aske was found guilty and sentenced to be hanged in chains from the battlements at York where he would die a slow, painful death from exposure and starvation.

A week later the Abbot of Fountains Abbey and a number of friars and monks were beheaded for treason and their heads set on London Bridge and the gates of London. Other abbots, priors, monks, priests and laymen were to follow them to the gallows.

With the ridings forcibly resettled, Yorkshire wool received its first recorded parliamentary recognition.

The county was achieving a reputation for making bed coverlets, in a type of stout (worsted) fabric; the business was sufficiently important to the local economy in terms of trade and jobs that an appeal was made to parliament for a Norwich-style monopoly in the production of bedclothes. The application on behalf of the Guild of Coverlet Makers (formed in York around 1400) was successful, with an Act in 1542 of which the preamble explains that:

> '...the city of York being one of the ancientest and greatest cities within the realm of England, and before this time hath been maintained and upholden by divers and sundry handicrafts there used, and most principally by making and weaving of coverlets and coverings for beds, and thereby a great number of the inhabitants and people of the said city and suburbs thereof, and other places within the county of York, have been daily set on work in spinning, dyeing, carding, and weaving of the said coverlets...

The act gave the 'exclusive' privilege of the making

and marketing of bed coverings to the city of York.

And yet the rebellious nature of the wool-working community had not dissipated. The crown still owned the common lands where sheep had been reared for centuries and it charged excessive rents for them. The high price of wool and provisions threated the existence of the poor spinners of Norfolk. Their discontent, fanned by hundreds of ejected monks, was attributed to the effects of both the destruction of their monasteries and the Reformation. In 1549 another furious rebellion broke out, led by Robert Kett, a tanner.

An estimated 16,000 people from Norfolk and surrounding counties sacked Norwich, driving out wealthy inhabitants, murdering foreigners and rendering the town virtually desolate. The insurrection was suppressed only after 5,000 of the rebels had been killed and Kett hanged.

The local industry had now been damaged beyond repair. According to one historian Norwich had been reduced to 'a resort of the idle and the dissolute'.

Its long primacy had been lost. The new era would become known as 'The Commotion Time'.

During the five years that Mary Tudor was on the throne her attempt to restore to the Church the property confiscated by Henry was largely thwarted by parliament.

She encouraged, and then compelled, a large number of Protestants, along with the refugees who had sought religious sanctuary under Henry, to leave the country 'for conscience's sake'. Most of them emigrated to Antwerp and set up, or resumed, business there. They did well to leave – she had nearly 300 religious dissenters burned at the stake.

Although the number of departing artisans was at first large enough to make a noticeable effect on the industry, the supply of wool product was sufficient to match home consumption during the latter part of her reign while export of it more or less ceased, owing to a decrease in the amount of wool available.

It is difficult to source the population of cities in those days – a figure of about 40,000 people has been reported as the number who worked in the allied weaving trades in the area of Norwich. But an Act of Parliament passed in those days may give a clue as to comparative figures: no city or town could have more than two taverns – except London, which was allowed 40, York could have eight, Bristol six, and Norwich four. Which might be interpreted to mean that York had twice the population of Norwich – or merely that it was considered twice as important, although population was much more likely to have been the deciding factor.

Boom Time for Looms

In the 14th century – after the Italians had stopped checking wool exports – the annual number of taxed sacks of raw wool had averaged about 30,000. By the end of the 15th century it had dropped below 9,000, and was less than 5,000 by 1550.

Meanwhile, as a partial result of the export embargo, weaving had increased and exports of English cloth had soared. Yorkshire pieces were being sold for tailoring in Germany, Gascony, Belgium, Portugal, Spain and the Low Countries. Worse, from the point of view of the traditional continental weavers, they were being imported at a price with which they could not compete.

In Bruges, which had been the biggest importer of raw wool to feed them, its 40,000 looms were at a virtual standstill. There was a similar situation at Ypres, and the entire weaving industry of the Low Countries started a gradual degeneration.

The Italians may have been making the finest quality clothing, using the finest (and most expensive) quality of wool, but... English cloth was not actually that bad, and it was a lot cheaper. The Tuscans started to pay more attention to their Chianti.

When Yorkshire weavers prospered so did the country, and the county's rural areas were enjoying a boom period.

Access to fast-flowing water to drive the fulling mills, cheap labour to comb and spin the raw wool, and a refusal to play along with the strict rules of the guilds about quality, patterns, apprenticeships, staffing, demarcation (who-does-what-job) disputes, working hours, and even directives for personal behaviour meant that the farmers of the West Riding could make hay by making cloth.

The Guild-controlled weaving townsfolk, saddled with their own restrictive practices, could not keep pace with their unfettered counterparts in the hills and dales.

The Guilds at least had a charitable nature. In 1567 and 1569 York set up weaving establishments to teach the trade to the unemployed, but the resultant cloth proved to be unsellable. In 1574 they set up classes for the handicapped to learn spinning, and five years later invested £400 in wool for the poor to work with. In 1597 a man from Hartlepool was provided with a rent-free house, an interest-free loan, a contract for ten years, plus freedom of the city of York as his reward for teaching aspects of the industry to the poor. The experiment came to nought. Similarly in 1619 a Norwich weaver of fine worsteds was employed to pass on his skills to the poor; he too was given the freedom of York, a house and a loan, but within a year the scheme had failed, and the investment was written off.

A much more modest project was started in the 1630s, with one local master being paid £20 a year to teach poor people how to spin yarn. This was the only experiment that would prove successful.

But by 1500, when 90% of the population worked, directly or indirectly 'on the land', three regional centres had emerged as textile producers: the West Country, East Anglia, and Yorkshire – which stole a march on the competition by its introduction of a more reliable system than waiting for the haphazard production of outsourced spinners.

Merchants became employers of spinners, and increased the scale of textile production by supplying wool yarn to the home weavers, and then unprocessed cloth to a network of home–based outworkers, who could perform most of the specialised finishing operations that were needed in the final production of textiles. The merchants had little else to do then, than take the cloth to market.

In 1563 the ancestors of Reuben Gaunt, who would become one of the most prominent textile-weaving mill owners in the Leeds–Bradford area, arrived from Ghent and started trading in wool.

The more enterprising West Riding weaver read the plot – and became a merchant himself. Now he sourced the yarn, and he put it out to spinners, then to weavers and finally to fullers, and he sold the pieces and paid the workers. He could work his own loom with a neighbour to keep it going when he was otherwise occupied; he could maybe fit an extra loom beside it, pay people to weave on it and keep an eye on their work. Or he could give neighbours the yarn to weave on their own looms. All he needed was yarn; he could pay women to spin it.

The West Riding trade soon superseded York and Beverley, the traditional weaving centres, which were hobbled by guild rules and higher prices. Their cloths may have been courser and the processes doubtless less sophisticated – it was still being said that, even when using the same wool as the west country's weavers, the Yorkshire product was inferior. But there was no shortage of it, and there was no shortage of variety or of colour. And it was cheap.

A tax survey in 1595 reported:
> At Wackefeilde, Leedes and some other smale villages nere thereabouts there is made about 30 packes of brode cloths every weecke, and ev'y packe is four whole clothes; the sortes made in Wackefeilde are tawnyes, browns, blues and some reddes; in Leedes of all colours..

In 1561 York council minutes bemoaned the exodus of the city's weavers to Halifax, Leeds and Wakefield – no doubt in order to escape the stranglehold of the local Guild.

Halifax started to dominate production of worsteds, becoming the largest cloth production centre in the West Riding, selling its produce all over the country. It would be found on stalls of the cloth halls at St Bartholomew's fair and at Blackwell Hall in London where it was bought for export. A tailor in York now offered cloths in Halifax Green, Halifax Tawny, Halifax Russet and Halifax Niger. In 1467 records show 14 men – including eight fullers – working wool in the town. The national fame and prosperity achieved by Halifax during the 15th and 16th centuries surprised the surrounding area and remains a source of pride for many of its townsfolk, to this day.

Uninhibited by any concern about finery or fashion, Halifax chose to concentrate on the production of 'Kersey' – a textile made from raw wool that had been carded, but not combed, producing a thick felted cloth that was hard-wearing, water-resistant and good value for inexpensive clothing. In 1613 it would be reported that the output of Kerseys alone in the Halifax area (it included parts of Bingley, Bradford and Keighley) was more than 90,000 pieces a year.

And as the quality gradually improved, so did its reputation, and consequently the start of the domination of the West Riding as the centre for the reliability of its reasonably priced textile products. Kerseys and 'Northern Dozens' (a slightly cheaper form of Kersey sold at a minimum length of 12 yards), were being sent to Hull or London for export to Germany, Poland and Russia, and were favoured for clothing by the monks of Durham and the choristers of Cambridge.

Although it was reckoned that one yard-wide piece of Northern Dozen could be woven by one man in one week the production of it, from beginning to end, might involve labour for 15 people. There was, therefore, no shortage of work in the area. People would travel from other parts of the country in search of jobs.

Leeds and Wakefield provided the main markets and thereby the main finance for the rest of the county and consequently became the places in which the more successful merchants made their homes. Wakefield developed as the centre for trading in the wool, and Leeds dominated the selling of the cloth.

The downside – there is usually a downside – was

that the rest of the country began, at last, to take notice of the West Riding, especially with regard to its industry and perceived wealth.

Towards the end of the 16th century the Queen (now Elizabeth I) ordered that every port, depending on its size, should maintain at least one ship, armed and victualled, fully manned and equipped, and ready for service at sea – either in home waters or abroad. Of course, this meant nothing to the only Riding without a coastline. Even Hull, and York (which had been designated as a 'port' only in order to enhance its importance, on the basis that the Ouse was navigable from the sea to the town), initially made little attempt to comply. But early in 1596, when Hull was ordered to produce a ship to join the expedition to Cadiz during the Anglo–Spanish war, the harbour authorities said they could not afford to supply and maintain such a vessel – unless the clothiers of the West Riding, the people who made most use of the port, contributed to the cost.

Hull identified 'the three great clothing towns' of Halifax, Leeds and Wakefield and, accordingly, a bill for £400 was dispatched to the clothing industry there, with a demand to pay their share.

With what was perhaps the first recorded, though semi–official, display of what would become seen as typical Yorkshiremen's solidarity and stubbornness, the order was ignored.

When the demand was repeated, a response was sent, refusing to pay, on the grounds that the clothiers belonged to 'only inland towns, bordering on no navigable river or haven', and that they had no responsibility for, nor any direct connection with, the port of Hull, and therefore were not subject to any form of tax levied on 'ports'.

The Privy Council accepted that this was a fair and reasonable response and the West Riding's tradespeople were officially 'excused from any payment whatsoever'. However, 'whatsoever' did not mean 'for ever': it was a concession applied only once.

At the end of the same year, Hull was hit by another levy or 'Ship Tax', for £1,400, and once again the shared responsibility was passed on to the clothiers. And, once again, they ignored it.

When the request was turned into a demand the local magistrates simply relayed the information to London that the inland towns refused to pay. The demands kept coming and they kept being ignored. A whole year passed. Eventually the Privy Council, frustrated, exasperated and angered by the disrespect clearly evident in the lack of any response, summoned the four leading magistrates of the area before them.

The justices were threatened that if they did not impose the levy they would have to make up all of any shortfall themselves. The West Riding clothiers, beaten but unbowed, coughed up 'fower hundreth poundes' towards the levy. The magistrates had done their honourable best, to support and represent them.

Taxes do not go away, and nor did the response of the cloth towns. In 1626 Hull was still complaining that

> we have sent sundry times to those of Halifax Leeds and Wakefield for their proportionable assistance...and yet we have received no monies...' '

The Wool/Cloth District was now a geographically recognisable entity. Its people were now an identifiable community. Its local magistrates had emerged as its champions in protecting its people in the best interests of their livelihoods.

By the end of the First Elizabethan Age, the West Riding may have become known for its stubbornness, and for its unwillingness to part too readily with its money – but more importantly it had achieved fame as a separate commonality and, incidentally, by now as the main supplier of cheap textiles for clothing most parts of the world.

Half a century later – the middle 1600s – Leeds was still a small town in real terms, controlling a rural population of around 4,000 (compared to York's 10,000). The town itself was little more than a triangle bordered by the River Aire, Briggate and Kirkgate, surrounded by open fields and meadows and patches of woodland.

Nevertheless, the merchants of Leeds had established themselves as the middlemen for all parts of the wool industry. They financed the travellers who bought raw wool and they sold the best of it – but ever diminishing amounts of it – to the foreign buyers who were still on hand waiting for it.

They then employed people to full and to spin the rest of it, selling yarn to under-employed farmer-weavers, and buying it back as cloth. Sometimes they simply supplied the wool for rural home–workers to weave for them, leaving a deposit and then paying the balance for the cloth – 'the piece rate' – when the job was done, or they bought ready-made pieces from Halifax, to sell on.

These entrepreneurs would then usually organise the 'finishing' (improving) and often the dyeing of the cloth, some of which – with relatively easy access to the port of Hull – they could ship down the east coast to tailors in the south of the country while concurrently controlling England's biggest source of foreign income: the exporting of good and cheap cloth.

The English worsted industry grew due to a vibrant home demand and, during the seventeenth century, it became the most dynamic element of overseas trade by overtaking its Dutch, Belgian and German competitors and by capturing the Mediterranean markets as the Italian and Spanish textile industries diminished in popularity.

The wool merchants of the West Riding had become the nation's first capitalists.

Defoe, writing about Yorkshire in 1727, reported that:

> ...every clothier must keep a horse, perhaps two, to fetch and carry for the use of his manufacture, to fetch home his wooll and his provisions from the market, to carry his yarn to the spinners, his manufacture to the fulling mill, and, when finished, to the market to be sold, and the like; so every manufacturer generally keeps a cow or two, or more, for his family, and this employs the two, or three, or four pieces of enclosed land about his house, for they scarce sow corn enough for their cocks and hens...
>
> Among the manufacturers houses are scattered an infinite number of cottages or small dwellings, in which dwell the workmen which are employed, the women and children of whom, are always busy carding, spinning, &. so that no hands being unemploy'd, all can gain their bread, even from the

youngest to the antient; hardly any thing above four years old, but its hands are sufficient to itself.

This is the reason also why we saw so few people without doors; but if we knock'd at the door of any of the master manufacturers, we presently saw a house full of lusty fellows, some at the dye- vat, some dressing the cloths, some in the loom, some one thing, some another, all hard at work, and full employed upon the manufacture, and all seeming to have sufficient business.

I should not have dwelt so upon this part, if there was not abundance of things subsequent to it, which will be explained by this one description, and which are needful to be understood by any one that desires a full understanding of the manner how the people of England are employed, and do subsist in these remoter parts where they are so numerous; for this is one of the most populous parts of Britain, London and the adjacent parts excepted.

While – before the 1700s – virtually every published record relating to the production of worsted referred to manufacture in the south, especially to Norfolk, the more modest folk of Yorkshire were busy at their looms.

It may be that they were unaware of the various laws (why would they bother about edicts designed for southerners?) or that they were in fact aware, but ignored them, on the basis that they did not apply to them, but only to those 'posh folk', down south.

While etymologists agree that the name comes from the Norfolk village, and date its first use as 1296, it was a familiar term in Yorkshire in 1310, where 'sayes of Worstede' – woollen blankets or cloaks – were recorded. And a will written in 1347 referred to *mon vieil lit d rouge worstede* ('my old red worsted bedcover').

More commonly, though, the county's weavers were concerned with making 'shalloon', a fabric that is defined in modern terms as a 'light, tightly woven *worsted*'.

This word comes from Châlons-sur-Marne (France) – since renamed as Châlons-en-Champagne – where it had originated as a type of weaving what would later become known as worsteds. The likelihood is that it came, not with the Flemish in Norfolk, but from the old conquerors of 1066 onwards, and that in Yorkshire they had been weaving 'worsteds' without knowing it and without the lawmakers being aware.

Yorkshire's problem from the start had been the shortage of long-haired fleeces with which to make fine textiles. For the most part, its weavers were satisfied with making kerseys, a type of rough woollen cloth produced from inferior fleeces. The back of the cloth was napped and shorn after fulling, producing a dense, warm fabric with a smooth back. By 1475 the West Riding – mostly around Halifax – had become the major producer.

The cloth was popular among the working classes and was in great demand for military uniforms. During both the English and the American Civil Wars both sides wore uniforms made of kersey. So did the Kaiser's German forces and the Tsar's imperial army.

The name derives almost certainly from the village of Kersey, Suffolk, having presumably originated in that region. Or it may have been brought to England by the Normans. In Old English it meant 'watercress'.

Even more likely, however, would have been the natural realisation that strands of long fine sheep wool – separated from the short and crimped fibres – combed gently and put into parallel lines for twisting and spinning, produced a better quality, and therefore a more highly priced product. The problem remained that long-haired sheep were rare in Yorkshire. It is perhaps a reasonable conjecture that, while most of the country's nobility was clothed by East Anglia, most of its hoi polloi was dressed by the West Riding.

Over the centuries Yorkshire wool producers had cross- bred their flocks with long-haired sheep mainly from Lincolnshire, providing the opportunity to weave a greater quantity of 'shalloons' (or worsteds).

Otherwise, it is anybody's guess as to how the principal seat of weaving (weaving of any kind) shifted from Norwich and ended in Bradford.

It is vital to remember that nobody, beyond family members who passed down their knowledge (weaving from father to son, spinning from mother to daughter), was teaching the various arts of cloth making. There were no night schools, no colleges of arts and crafts. Weavers worked quickly – even more so when they adapted the loom left by the Romans from a vertical to horizontal position. They realised that they could make broader cloth if a friend stood at the other side and passed the shuttle back.

Although some men made a profession of spinning, the word 'spinster' would eventually evolve to describe 'a woman who spins'.

It is reckoned that a good spinner or spinster would produce about half a pound of wool a day. In Skipton, in 1785, young women spun for 12 hours in a spinning contest and the winner produced 1.6 lbs of good quality wool, which made the newspapers as 'an extraordinary instance of exertion in the art of spinning'.

It was, indeed, extraordinary: one pound in weight of fine wool could produce ten miles of yarn.

Weaver, 1698, with a man combing, at left.

The Maister

Once a man decided that he could make money if he concentrated on weaving, he would be aware that there were so many other aspects involved in the process of achieving a finished piece of cloth that he needed to call in friends and neighbours to assist him.

The paterfamilias would teach his son all of 'the necessary mysteries' as his formal apprentice for at least seven years after which the son could also call himself a weaver and be legally entitled to sell cloth. Neighbours could have been recruited to lend a hand with the preparation: cleaning, carding or combing, and spinning in return for payment. After all, not every family was devoted to sheep farming. There were small–scale cereal growers (and labourers) and there were cattle farmers (and labourers) and leather workers (and labourers) working on the sheep skins. There were carpenters and wheelwrights and housebuilders and butchers and bakers... And their wives... And, throughout history, there were people with no real jobs at all.

The man who organised the weaving into a local industry was called the master, or 'maister'. Trades and skills evolved from this. Some villagers – of both sexes – would be happy to do only wool-sorting, only carding (separating the fibres), or only spinning, taking in work as it was offered. In a small village virtually any part of the process could effectively become a full-time job with the amount of wool being shorn at the start of every summer.

Some men who wanted to work at home alone would take up spinning and in the Yorkshire Dales about a quarter of the men would have described their job as 'spinner'. The introduction of the pedal-powered spinning wheel may seem obvious today, but it took the Italians to invent it and the English to copy it. Allowing the spinner to work with both hands (instead of with one hand turning the wheel) more than doubled the speed of the task.

Wages and prices for this period are extremely difficult to find but in the 1380s decent wool, woven, would fetch five shillings (60 pence) a yard. To put this into some sort of context, you could get two dozen eggs or two chickens for a penny.

These skills developed into vital income-generating trades in the clusters of cottages that would slowly develop into 'wool towns'. Farming families could take their wool to be carded and spun, for a price, freeing them for their own domestic tasks.

Four different types of family evolved: there were the shepherds, producing wool that they would sell; the farmers, who did a bit of weaving when they found time for it; the weavers, who farmed as a side-line and the weavers who did nothing but weaving.

These last were the small 'independent clothiers', often retaining small freeholds that the family would run, who made cloth on a modest scale and would be the backbone of the industry until around the 1850s – about a century after the West Riding had virtually monopolised the wool industry.

They had their own spinning wheels and looms and could manage most of the processes themselves. The weaver bought his wool at the market, his wife and children usually carded and spun it, and if they were unable to keep up with his pace neighbours would be recruited to assist with the different processes. Assisted by his son, as the apprentice, the maister would dye his wool, weave his piece of cloth, pay to have it fulled and take it – in its 'unfinished' state – to his stall in the marketplace or his stand in the cloth hall.

Cottage spinner, 1814

From his profits he paid for any outside work, a fee to the fulling mill – and bought a new quantity of wool in order to start the process all over again.

The maister was his own man. His profits were the

makings of his own family's labour: a justifiable source of pride. It did not, however, make them rich. Working long hours a man and his son would be hard pushed to produce more than one piece a week (although some of them managed two) but, living frugally as smallholders, with between three and 15 acres of land, they could at least live in a degree of comfort.

Although most of them would own a horse or ass to convey their pieces to market, it was a common sight to see the poorer weavers carrying their wares on their head or shoulders. John Mayhall (writing in 1848) even identifies one such horseless clothier as Richard Wilson, of Ossett, who carried a piece of wool on his head for about ten miles to Leeds Cloth Hall where he sold it to a merchant who said he would be more than happy to buy more of the same. Maister Wilson asked his customer to wait. He walked back home, where he picked up a second piece which he conveyed to the merchant's warehouse, before returning to Ossett – a day's walking of nearly 40 miles, half of it with a bolt of cloth on his head.

It was obvious to any canny Yorkshireman that he could set up, or set up his son, when qualified, in a family business that cut out the middlemen – the buyers of wool and the merchants of pieces – by doing most of the processes for manufacturing unfinished wool themselves. All that was needed was the price of the original fleeces. Any fees that were accrued along the way were credited until the piece was sold at market.

Big merchants did their business in the Cloth Halls, small timers could also trade there, but they could also sell in the town market. The weavers were in business. They brought their friends in with them and put their looms together, in one building. Other weavers got the idea and formed 'weaving clubs' that could keep looms working round the clock. Weavers would 'sign on', marking the start of their shift by writing their initials in chalk on the fabric; this way their contribution to a finished piece could be calculated for proportionate payment.

They accumulated wealth – not great wealth, by any means, but more than they had been used to – by buying wool and finding larger premises with the accumulated profits, installing more looms...

...They were inventing 'the mill'.

But these were necessarily small projects. There was no capital available to tenant farmers for the purchase or the erection of large buildings.

Nevertheless, the weaving industry, which within the Riding produced mainly kerseys (the weaving of worsteds, as such, would not start until about a century later) required a beginning and an end.

The beginning was finding fleeces, and the raw wool.

The front-line operators were those who grew the product and weaved it themselves, even if they had to call in friends to help. There was always the possibility that they would weave more than they grew, in which case they would need to become wool buyers, as well as shepherds and weavers.

The end was with the maister: seeking the best wool and buying it, getting it cleaned, carded or combed, paying for the spinning, equipping the weaving, organising the fulling, and getting the textile pieces to market for sale.

A prime example was Abimelech Hainsworth who, as a teenager, bought a piece of cloth for half-a-crown, sold it for a profit, bought another, and sold it, and so on until, he was able to take over the ailing Cape of Good Hope scribbling and fulling mill on the Bagley Beck, a tributary of the Aire, in Bramley. He later added a weaving shed to the site and is still remembered at Hainsworth's and locally as 't'auld maister',

Most of the industry, though, remained home-based. It was then the job of the maister to control the distribution of the raw material and equitably dole out the proceeds after sale.

Nevertheless, the industry in West Yorkshire would remain small-scale for hundreds of years. It was a relief from poverty, but not much more. And the maister would remain tied to his roots, retaining at least a small farm, and more than likely his own small flock of sheep.

Their looms – they worked faster than most domestic spinners could produce yarn – often risked standing idle for short periods, so they had to buy wool from middlemen who were always tempted to export it for a higher price. Their need for a quick return meant selling it quickly, at local markets… where a different type of middleman would buy it to sell on, elsewhere, at a higher price.

According to one (1588) source – describing a never-fulfilled plan to have 60 clothiers employed under one roof in Skipton – it was one full week's work for at least six people, buying sorting, carding, spinning, weaving and shearing, to make one piece of undyed kersey.

During the 16th century the average output of a West Riding weaver was reckoned to be one piece of kersey a week – provided only that the start and the finishing processes were carried out for him.

Enter Randall Tenche, a Leeds clothier of no little importance in the first Elizabethan age, who history seems to have largely overlooked.

He appears to have achieved some prominence as a dyer of precision, having made a deal with Sir Francis Willoughby of Wollaton Hall, near Nottingham, who was engaged in fancy cloth-making ventures, for:

> 'the dyeing and the spinning work of all sorts which he is emboldened to do, more especially as he has found out a workman or two who will join with him or be under him who will work any work that shall be set unto them by a painter in colours, and to work the same in woollen yarn...'

For this work Tenche received £50 a year and his workmen 6s 8d a week. In those days, a loaf of bread cost twopence and a chicken was a penny. Best beef was 3d a pound and a tankard of ale a half-penny. Lodging at an inn (including laundry) cost twopence a night. Broadcloth cost £6 for 24 feet.

Privy Council records show that in 1590 Tenche wrote, claiming 'the full consent of all the clothiers of the North partes':

> 'By reason of a corrupt practice of a great number of broggers, engrocers, regratours and such like' all the wool of the county had been snatched up and could be obtained by clothiers only at 'prisses exceedingly enhaunced and increased.'

[A brogger was a broker; an engrocer was (presumably) a retail merchant; a regrater buys from a producer to take a product to market.] Tenche pleaded for a vigorous enforcement of the law involving middlemen in the wool trade.

The Privy Council appointed him – 'a man of honest conversation and good skill and experience in such cases' – to check 'evil practices' in the West Riding.

There appear to have been many such reasons for concern about fair trading. The first in the system was the shepherds' practice of marking their own sheep with pitch or tar in a way that they could recognise them as being distinct from their neighbours' flocks. The tar was difficult to remove – and much heavier than the wool to which it was attached. The staplers who bought by the fleece, usually bought the tar with it, but when they sold by weight their buyers would refuse to take it into account.

Some wool cloth was sold wet, or damp, which added to the weight.

Other buyers found that their woolsacks contained clay, dust, sand or even stones. Some even started to demand that for every 28 lbs of cloth they paid for, they would receive 29 lbs, to cover predictable underselling.

Then there were cloths that were narrower, or shorter, than they were purported to be.

So Tenche was also later tasked with the duty of ensuring the quality of cloth, with power to seize any pieces that did not comply with the law. He was apparently so thorough that in 1598 many clothiers complained to the Wakefield Quarter Sessions against his seizure of their cloth.

Not a good idea: the court issued warrants for all

the appellants to appear before it to be penalised for their failings.

Tenche lived on a small plot of land, probably used for tentering cloth, between the river and Leeds parish church, where he was a churchwarden. But, sadly, little more of the detail is known about his work to improve the quality of making West Riding cloth and of the diligence he applied to his duties.

Such improvements as were made to the actual mechanical structure of the weaving industry came more from natural logic than from any form of innovatory progress. Two men – one at each side – could work a loom faster than one. The invention of the flying shuttle enabled those two men to work one loom each. An increasing population meant an increase in demand. If the weavers put their looms into one place, and maybe worked shifts – effectively forming their own small 'mills' – they could meet the demand. But more weaving meant a demand for more yarn to be spun, and more yarn required more fleeces being combed or carded locally, then with more yarn being produced, more weaving time was required to consume it.

The broad cloth, either in its full length of 24 yards, or as a ' Dozen ' of 12-13 yards, represented the highest grade of Northern fabrics. It was made of the best wool, chiefly drawn from Lincolnshire or other counties. Next in order of value was the kersey, which was only slightly lower in quality than the broad, but longer and not so wide. It was made of the same brands of wool as the Dozen, and sold at 1s 6d to 2s 6d per yard in the early seventeenth century, when broads sold at 4s to 5s. These two cloths were the staples of the Yorkshire industry and export trade.

The weavers were doing very well, thank you. The toil was hard and intensive, but it worked. And if the system and the equipment wasn't broken, you didn't fix it.

Until well into the 19th century – in spite of the best efforts of established guilds – there was no form of organisation of the majority of spinners or weavers, who in many cases were occupied with wool only in their spare time, after their main agricultural labour. Wool provided a supplementary, rather than a main income, for many who saw it as a form of immunity from a poor harvest.

Historians, apparently, call this type of system 'proto–industrialisation': rural peasants usually working from home for lower remuneration than urban artisans who worked in factories or mills..

The rest of us call it cottage industry.

Dyeing for the Country

The monarchy (including Henry VIII, except when his tailors could source him cloth of gold) preferred coats in bright red, known as 'stammel'. Consequently, so did the nobility.

The peasantry wore a different shade, identified as 'russet', a mixture of woad and madder that produced a browner shade of red with an orange tinge. It had been an identifier of the poorer classes since the mid-1300s.

Since 1463 the wearing of 'royal purple' – a term which, during the Middle Ages, referred not only to purple but also to crimson, dark reds and 'royal blue' – had been restricted to the nobility.

The problem for the aristocrats was that, in spite of the number of dyehouses in the country and the number of tradesmen who were named (as in Tinctor or Tynctor, Lister, Dyer and Dexter) for their occupations, dyeing in England was still an experimental craft: the dye-masters had the basic colours, but not the consistency. The finest woven worsted fabrics were therefore dispatched abroad for more expert dyeing and finishing in bright red, and then reshipped to England for tailoring. The same process was applied for the better qualities of greens, blues and blacks.

Working class and middle class taste, meanwhile,

was influenced more by the climate and the simplicity of style than by fashionable colours. Customers wanted a thick and heavy cloth – durable, soft, pliable and warm – which meant wool or silk. And the majority favoured, and could afford, wool. If the market was for the plain but substantial, Yorkshire could provide for it. The product may have been somewhere south of mediocrity. But the industry was going for quantity rather than quality.

Dyers had to be licensed but did not necessarily have any sole-right privileges – there could be several within one area. However, in 1352 when Walter Lister, a dyer from Leeds, was fined four shillings for practising in Bradford without a licence he reacted by applying for the 'office of dyer for Bradeforddale', thereby effectively securing a monopoly for dyeing within the manor – in return for an annual fee… of four shillings.

There was, at that time, a mill in Leeds with similar monopolistic terms, leased at 20 shillings per year.

Dyeing was also a cottage industry, or part of one, and spinners with mixed colours among their fleeces would often dye them with 'natural' colour or bleach them to give the expression of consistency, at least within a single piece. It was called being 'dyed in the wool', as distinct from being dyed after weaving: 'dyed in the cloth'.

As with weaving, Yorkshire's yarn spinners were not best known for the quality of their dyeing. Apparently, they did not change the mixture sufficiently frequently. Buyers reported that some of the dyed product was 'muddy', even 'dung-coloured'. Achieving 'russet' – an inexact shade in any case – was therefore not much of a challenge for Yorkshire dyers.

In September 1643 Oliver Cromwell wrote:

> 'I had rather have a plain, russet– coated captain that knows what he fights for, and loves what he knows, than that which you call a gentleman and is nothing else.'

The natural colour of a typical sheep, and of its fleece, often appears to be pure white, but when spun it most likely shows traces of the faintest brown, a sort of pale nicotine, in its strands. (The French invented the word *beige* for it, particularly for the, usually stained, underparts of a sheep.) So the owner of the length of spun wool had to decide whether to increase its value, either by bleaching or by dyeing.

We know, from ancient sources, that stale human urine is an effective whitener. Cow urine – somebody discovered – will turn wool yellow. Presumably there would be no shortage of that liquid on most farms, provided only that a method could be found of collecting it.

Woad, as we also know, produced blue. It was a colour most favoured in the big wool–producing town of Coventry. It was so well fixed into the cloth – it took about three days soaking to make a colour that was 'fast' – that it claimed the distinction of being 'true blue', an expression that would come to mean reliable (not a word often used to describe dyers in other wool towns). It may be why the two oldest universities chose blue as their 'colours'.

Crimson came from the root of the madder plant (*rubia tinctorum*) and had been used in the wrappings of the mummified body of Tutankhamun (about 1327BC), and much later in the redcoats of the British army and for the coats of countrymen's 'hunting pink'.

Chestnut shells could produce colours from peach to brown. Tree bark – also used for 'tanning' the leather sheepskins – gave a gentle pinkish hue.

There was no shortage of experimentation and discovery in dye opportunities. But a colour needed to be decided upon and it needed to be consistent. Whether the hanks or skeins of wool were coloured before or after weaving, the wool had to be simmered over constant heat for hours (sometimes for days) until it was clear to the dyer that the colour was right and that it was fully absorbed. It needed to be a constituent part of the wool, not merely a coating of the fibres.

To fix it – stale human urine, again. The fungus that grew on oak trees also worked for fixing, as did vinegar.

There was a good reason why dyeing was a process usually carried out on the (downwind) edges of a village, usually alongside leather-tanning works – the other sheep product – which also used stale urine for softening and dyeing.

Then, rinsing again. A source of constant fresh running water was vital to the industry.

In most cases, merchants trading in medium to finer quality cloth supervised their own dyeing and finishing, including cloth–shearing, often in outbuildings of their own houses.

They also had the option of using specialised dye-houses which were, at the time, the main smoke-producing industries in Leeds.

Dyehouses were generally located along the River Aire or the Sheepscar, a stream that flowed into the Aire in the east of the town.

But English dyers did not (so to speak) 'win their colours' over subsequent centuries.

During the First Elizabethan period, soldiers started to be dressed in scarlet coats and, as the uniformity spread, so did the variety of 'scarlets'. The fact that English (and later British) soldiery was virtually permanently at war would mean plenty of steady work for the weaving industry. It mattered little that the soldiers' coats may have been in different shades of red, so long as it remained obvious to riflemen which side they were supposed to shoot at.

A Parliament of Owls

Charles II (1660-1685), something of a snappy dresser himself, imposed an absolute prohibition on the export of fleeces to foreign weavers. It was an Act which, frequently reinforced by subsequent statutes, would remain in force until 1825.

From the Restoration to the end of the 17th century the textile industry suffered a period of stagnation as those countries that had been buying English cloth started weaving for themselves with English wool.

William III (1689-1702) drew up elaborate plans for a naval patrol along the Yorkshire coast, as well as a surveyor and a team of 18 fast riders to prevent illegal movement of fleeces on land in the vicinity of ports and even of narrow creeks.

In 1702 a House of Lords Commission had reported that

> 'In divers foreign countries, France, Holland, Flanders, Spain, Portugal, Sweden, Silesia, Luneburg and other parts of Germany, new manufactures have been set up, which we take to be another reason why our trade in woollen has not been further enlarged.'

In 1703 the merchant clothiers of Leeds complained:

> 'the Woollen manufacture doth sensibly decline in several branches particularly in the vending thereof into fforaigne countreys.'

And according to Treasury papers of the time the burghers of Halifax reminded the king:

> Upon the Woollen Manufactures and Trade depends in a great Measure the Wealth of Your Majesty's kingdome, the Imployment of the poor and the Incouragement of Navigation which Trade is Decayed of Late in these Northerne partes.

A similar note was received from Wakefield.

Various attempts were made to revive the textile trade – and not for the first time. As far back as Henry III (1216 to 1272) Parliament had decreed that everyone 'should use woollen cloth made within the country'.

A 1571 Act of Parliament to stimulate domestic wool consumption had decreed that on Sundays and holidays, all males over six years of age, except for the nobility and persons of degree, were to wear woollen caps on pain of a fine of three farthings (¾ of a penny) per day. This law instituted the woollen 'flat cap' as part of English wear. It was repealed in 1597.

During the depressions of the reign of James I (target of the Gunpowder Plot in 1605) many people complained that the wearing of silks and foreign fabrics was displacing the traditional English woollens, and they clamoured for legislation to compel the wearing of English woollen cloths in preference to these fancy and foreign materials.

A less likely proposal, which was embodied into a statute of 1666, was an Act 'for the encouragement of the Woollen Manufacture of the Kingdom', demanding that

> 'noe person shall be buryed in any Shirt... or Sheete, made of or mingled with Flax, Hemp, Silk, Haire, Gold or Silver, or other than what shall be made of Wooll onely... or be putt into any

> Coffin lined or faced with anything made or mingled with Flax, Hemp, &c, upon paine of the forfeiture of the Summe of Five pounds, to be imployed to the use of the Poore of the Parish where such person shall be buryed,'

It seemed to be a difficult law to check, or to monitor, and was replaced twelve years later by a much more formidable decree, which directed that a register should be kept in every parish in which someone had to certify that everything in the coffin, apart from the corpse, was made of sheep's wool. The Act, reinforced in 1680, remained on the Statute Book until the nineteenth century. Entries in accordance with its clauses and instances of its infringement may occasionally be encountered in local parish registers, and generally run as follows (Richmond Quarter Sessions, 1679):

> Fine of five pounds levied on the goods of Thomas Norton, late deceased and buried in the Bedale Parish Church, no certificate having been made to the Rector of Bedale within eight days of the buriall that the said Thomas was buried in wool according to the Statute.

But encouraging the use of wool to support the wool industry was for nothing, if the wool itself was being exported.

For years, beating the authorities became something of a game, possibly even being seen (by non–players) as romantic, like smuggling, only in reverse. It was known as 'Owling', presumably because it involved taking flight by night.

Ingenious plans were considered by parliaments, from the 'registration' of all wool, immediately it was sheared, to the idea of building vast warehouses to which all fleeces should be taken, to be graded, valued and distributed. The merchants of Leeds were not so keen on that idea, or that any movement of wool should be banned in coastal areas – and they were especially opposed to the suggestion that the entire English wool clip should become the property of the state, and be issued to the English weavers as and when they needed it.

In fact, any idea was open to official consideration, if it could stop the export of English wool to foreign looms.

Yorkshire's raw-wool dealers quickly realised that if they crossed the Cheviots with their fleeces, the numerous ports of Scotland were beyond the control of English coastguards.

France was the main destination, especially for long wool, which was apparently rarer across the Channel, and vital for making worsteds. Travelling English writers of the period reported seeing packs of contraband being unloaded at ports like Dunkirk, and of the use of good English wool keeping the looms of France and Holland busy. One writer bemoaned

> 'the existence of the traitor who would so far sink his patriotism as to carry away supplies of long wool to the perfidious foe.'

In 1742 and 1767 Leeds Corporation appealed to the House of Commons to give its earnest attention towards

> 'preventing the pernicious practice of running our Wooll from Great Britain into foreign countrys'.

But continental countries wanted wool, not cloth, in order to maintain their own weaving industries. Austria imposed heavy duties on the import of cloth; the Regent of Hanover decreed in 1756 that all Hanoverian troops who had previously been kitted out in Yorkshire cloth should wear 'Hanoverian fabrics only'. The growth of clothmaking in the German states was a constant source of uneasiness to English dealers, who were afraid that one of their best markets would slip from their grasp.

Yorkshire cloths were especially suited for military uniforms and had been favoured by many European governments until the rise of native industries which dispensed with the need for woven imports. Peter the Great was another who aimed for the cultivation of a textile industry in Russia, in order to clothe his armies.

But the 1770s saw a turnround in production; better sheep-breeding and closer attention to sheep rearing had started to increase the amount of wool available, and yarn was also being imported from Irish sheep. A sudden surplus brought down the price of wool. In 1775 it cost 8½d a pound; by 1779 it had dropped to 6d. The merchants now had masses of wool that they could not sell at a profit.

Lincolnshire's wool men had an inspired, even if audacious, idea that since their product demanded a higher price when sold (illegally) abroad, they would apply for a licence to export 'small quantities' to Europe.

Yorkshire weavers – who preferred the long-fibred Lincolnshire wool to their local clip – had by this time formed what they called the Worsted Committee, and rigorously opposed that idea. The government appeared sympathetic to the problems of over-production, even suggesting that Lincolnshire shepherds might be better employed by turning their moorland pastures into arable land and growing flax or hemp, perhaps even with government subsidies. The shepherds rejected that and Parliament rejected the request for export licences.

So it was back to smuggling. Government spies were employed, paid by a percentage of imposed fines or seizures. In 1784 customs men seized 42,000lbs of wool at English ports, although vast quantities evaded the officials: some was boarded on ships labelled as hops; some was rowed out on small boats on moonless nights to ships moored at a distance offshore. It was said that ships rarely left Yorkshire and Lincolnshire ports without a few packs of wool hidden in the holds. The West Riding worsted men were furious about the Owlers constantly defeating the spies and customs men, and demanded more stringent attention, along with more stringent punishment.

In 1787 a new Act made any person concerned in any way with the export of wool liable to a fine of £3 for every pound weight discovered and to three months of solitary confinement for a first offence, with six months for any subsequent offence, along with the forfeiture of all ships, boats and carriages involved. Regulations were introduced to control the movement of wool across county lines (it was allowed between Lincolnshire and Yorkshire).

According to the *Leeds Intelligencer*, when the new laws were passed there was great rejoicing by workmen in all the Yorkshire clothing towns; church bells were rung, speeches were made, and bonfires lighted the sky at night.

While it is impossible to judge just how successful the new law could have been, it certainly had popular support, and the Worsted Committee and its supportive justices worked hard to get smugglers into the dock.

In 1788 Edmund Barker of Thorne was sentenced to three months at York for exporting wool from the East Riding to Dunkirk. He was fined £3 for every pound, and his 'goods and chattels' were seized. [Barker, as a surname, has two possible roots: either a tanner of leather, using tree bark, or a shepherd, from the Old French *berchier*.]

In the same year three Swedish ships, said to have been exporting 1,300 pounds weight a year, were seized at Hull.

In 1789 Hainsworth and Son, a Leeds merchant (whose descendants may – or may not – have been the company that survives today as one of only two vertical mills) was found guilty of illegal packaging and export of fleeces.

The home supply of wool was important to the weaver, but in Yorkshire the clothiers preferred wool from Lincoln and Leicester breeds which had far heavier fleeces and longer fibres for their worsteds. Yorkshire's shorter fibres were better suited for the woollen trade.

Until about 1770 no serious attention had been paid to the improvement of sheep breeding and the average fleece of a sheep reared on common land rarely weighed more than 3½ pounds. Even that was an improvement on 1641 when *Rural Economy* reported that 'usually six of our fleeces make a just stone' (14 lb).

At the end of the 18th century John Luccock, a wool-stapler from Leeds, reported that the fleeces of

Yorkshire wool were small in weight, very dirty and were 'generally used in the district where they were produced, never going out of the county'.

But when attention started to be paid to the skills of sheep-rearing the weight of some Yorkshire's moorland fleeces doubled by the end of the 1700s and some others weighed in at 10 lb. However, sheep need grass...

A story is told of a shepherd in the early 1800s who, when asked by Sir John Sinclair, a writer on agriculture, how many sheep he kept to an acre, replied: 'Why, man, ye start at wrong end. Ye should ax how many acres to a sheep.'

Apparently the moorland ratio had become one sheep to eight acres.

Cloth Halls

Industry in Leeds was diversified – it would become known as 'the city with a thousand trades' – and in addition to worsted included linen, canvas, flax, carpets, blankets, glass and earthenware. It also evolved as a city of commerce, trading virtually anything – although its major trading was in woollen cloth.

By 1700, wool textiles accounted for 26 per cent of English manufacturing output, bigger than both metals and mining. Estimates of the workforce employed in the English wool industry rely on parish records which are unreliable and may have been exaggerated, but could have been as high as 1,500,000 people – which, if correct, meant that a quarter of the population was directly or indirectly involved in wool production. [The population of England and Wales at the start of the century was 6.1 million.]

The problem was that the manufacture and sale of the product was also diversified geographically, being carried out all over the place, quite literally.

As a rough guide, Leeds was the north-eastern limit of the clothing area. A line drawn between Airedale and Wharfedale would mark the northern boundary, while a more awkward boundary, passing from Leeds south to Wakefield, and then turning south-west towards

Huddersfield, would mark the southern limit.

'Not a single manufacturer is to be found more than one mile east or two miles north of Leeds,' according to the *Leeds Guide* of 1707. Chapel Allerton, now part of Leeds, was 'entirely outside the clothing district', and there was 'scarcely a single manufacturer of cloth to be found in the whole village'. Barwick-in-Elmet and neighbouring villages were as far beyond the clothing area as was the 'quietest little village in the Vale of York, being solely agricultural'. The qualification 'scarcely' allows for the likelihood that, even the 'quietest' little villages possibly, or probably, were making some sort of contribution, possibly spinning, or weaving, but on a small scale.

In fact, throughout almost the whole of the North and East Ridings there were some people involved in the manufacture of the finished cloth. Around Ripon and Middleham there was a considerable 'manufactory' of woollen goods or preparation of yarn that was either sent from the Dales to be woven in the West Riding or made into woollens at Masham and Middleham, or into carpets at Ripon, or into knitted goods in Wensleydale and Swaledale. Women in the East Riding prepared linen yarn, and in Cleveland they spun worsted, and used it for knitting. At Richmond, Daniel Defoe found

> 'a manufactory of knit–yarn stockings for servants and ordinary people. Every family is employed in this way, both great and small.'

Having been prepared, spun, knitted or woven, the stuff needed to be sold.

It might seem logical to assume that ancient pubs or inns with names like the Woolpack or the Fleece would be where the wool dealers operated in smaller and only local markets, although in Bradford – still little more than a small geographically handy marketplace with very little weaving of its own – the trade centred around the White Lion inn. (Addingham village had the Fleece – only because it was a wool 'town'. But it also had the Sailor and the Swan and the Craven Heifer, on its Main Street.)

Textile merchants (the buyers of the cloth being traded) often travelled great distances and needed to know when and where goods would be available for inspection and purchase, rather than calling hopefully at the homes of individual weavers. The business needed some sort of centralisation so that traders could buy when the pieces were ready. They did not want to arrive 'late' and find that the best materials had been sold; nor did the (mostly self-employed) weavers want to forsake good loom time and hang about in the hope that merchants would show up at some stage to buy. Both buyers and sellers required a fixed place, a fixed day, and even a fixed time of day.

In Leeds the business was at first out-of-doors, twice a week, on Tuesdays and Saturdays, but only in the mornings. Weavers set out their stalls, originally on the bridge across the Aire and later extended along Briggate, which was the main street running from it, a wide unpaved thoroughfare of narrow houses, made of wood and thatch. (The only brick house had been built for Thomas Metcalf, a wool merchant, at what would become a junction of Upper Headrow and Lands Lane.)

Briggate (YEP)

In 1719, when the Leeds merchants heard that a rival, and covered, market had been set up in Wakefield, about a dozen miles to the south, but further than some weavers wanted to travel with their cloth once or twice a week, they erected their own Cloth Hall in Kirkgate, the oldest street. By the mid-century it was outgrown and a Coloured Cloth Hall was opened at the junction of Park Row and (what would become) Wellington Street, at what is now City Square, with 1,800 stands or stalls, typically attracting 3,000 buyers of unfinished dyed cloth from the home weavers who brought their wares in on Tuesdays and Saturdays.

The building was 127 yards long and 66 yards broad, divided internally into 'streets', with stalls on either side.

Later still came a New Cloth Hall, opposite the Coloured Hall, handling the market in coarse woollens made in and around Batley. In 1810 an additional floor was added to the Coloured Cloth Hall, principally for the sale of undyed pieces that were perceived as being more suitable for women's apparel.

In order 'to promote regularity and expedition' the individual halls were open for only an hour and a quarter on each trading day, and transactions in that short period were recorded at up to £20,000 (in the early 1800s).

The Coloured Cloth Hall opened at 8.30am in summer, 9 o'clock in spring and autumn, and 9.30 in autumn. The White Cloth Hall opened when the Coloured Hall closed. However, because the weavers could leave their unsold materials within their rooms or lockers in the halls, trading would often be continued by promissory notes in exchanges at the Griffin Hotel on Boar Lane.

Both white and coloured cloth in Leeds was sold unfinished – leaving the dyeing, cropping and burling processes of the pieces to be arranged separately by the buyer. Gradually the buyers became Leeds residents, travelling out to sell their cloth, rather than travelling in, to buy it. They would often do the finishing of the pieces in the outhouses of their own homes. Coloured cloth would generally have been dyed in the wool, before the spinning, weaving and finishing.

Recorded sales rose from 30,000 pieces in the late 1720s to 60,000 pieces in the 1740s. In 1812 (the year that America declared war with England and Napoleon invaded Russia) dyed blue cloth could fetch 16 shillings a yard in the Leeds Coloured Cloth Hall.

Leeds was expanding dramatically: it now covered 60 acres; the population doubled between 1666 and 1731, and again doubled between 1760 and 1801.

As a finishing centre, and as a market for cloth, its prosperity advanced briskly. There was plenty of money available for building cloth halls, chapels, a theatre, and a library, while in one single year (1876) 400 dwellings were being built.

The conclusion of the American War reopened the American market, and the merchants of Leeds poured their goods into the new republic. When the struggle with France began, Yorkshire was flooded with orders from every part of Europe for fabrics for the clothing of troops. In 1797 a Mr Sheepshanks of Leeds was supplying scarlet and white cloth for the militia worth £1,400 a year, and in 1825 one Wakefield mill had been employing 400 hands for the past 20 years making broad cloths for the army.

The industry covered most parts of the county, with towns and villages still differentiated as textile, or non-textile, whether worsted or woollen, or white or mixed. Descending to a further subdivision, Wakefield still specialised in tammies, Leeds in broadcloths and in camlets, Halifax in shalloons and kerseys...

Halifax (about 20 miles south-west of Leeds) opened its Piece Hall in 1779 – a stunning monument to the grandeur of the wool industry and the only cloth hall still standing in Britain.

This coliseum had 315 rentable rooms for the general sale every Saturday morning (from 10am to noon) of its pieces, described as '30–yard lengths of fabric produced on a handloom of woven woollen kersey cloth'.

Since the 1400s the Calder Valley had become the predominant manufacturing base for this fabric that made use of thicker and more sturdy yarns of wool and was named after the Suffolk village that may have first produced it. It was recognised by its smooth (napped and sheared) back, producing a lighter-weight cloth, dense, warm, and with a smooth side closest to the skin of the wearer. It was later overtaken by 'serge'.

There did not appear to be many common rules for these cloth halls other than that, as an assurance of quality, one of the regulations of all halls was that only clothiers who had completed an apprenticeship could rent the stands. It was not easy to define an 'apprenticeship' though, as it included lads who had learnt to weave by working alongside their fathers.

And how long was a 'piece' of cloth? Apparently, the length varied – possibly according to the amount woven up to the time when the carrier was due to collect from the weaver and deliver it to the appropriate hall. Some pieces could be only 16 yards while others were more than 60.

Between 1724 and 1727, Daniel Defoe visited the cloth markets of Wakefield, Halifax and Leeds and asked what happened to all the cloth sold in them: 'where all these goods are vented and disposed of'.

The value of Defoe's writing is that he was one of the few travel writers of his time who actually visited the places he wrote about. Another is that he was a living witness to the Yorkshire cloth trade of 300 years ago. He offered to 'describe the consumption, for there are three channels by which it goes.'

These are his [edited] conclusions:

> First, for home consumption: their goods being everywhere made use of for clothing the ordinary people, who cannot go to the price of the fine medley of cloths made in the western counties of England.
>
> There are for this purpose a set of travelling merchants in Leeds, who go all over England with droves of pack horses, and to all the fairs and market towns over the whole island, I think I may say none excepted. Here they supply, not the common people by retail, which would denominate them pedlars, but the shops, by wholesale of whole pieces. They give large credit too, so that they are really travelling merchants, and as such they sell a very great quantity of goods.
>
> It is ordinary for one of these men to carry a thousand pounds value of cloth with them at a time, and having sold it at the fairs or towns where they go, they send their horses back for as much more.
>
> This occurs most often in a summer, when they choose to travel, and perhaps towards the winter time, tho' as little in winter as they can, because of the badness of the roads.
>
> Another sort are those who buy to send to London; either by commissions from London, or they give commissions to factors and warehouse–keepers in London to sell for them; and these also drive a very great trade.
>
> These factors and warehouse–keepers not only supply all the shop–keepers and wholesale men in London, but sell also very great quantities to the merchants, as well for exportation to the English colonies in America, which take off great quantities of those course goods, especially New England, New York, Virginia – and also to Russia merchants, who send an exceeding quantity to Petersburg, Riga, Dantzig, Narva, and to Sweden and Pomerania.
>
> The third sort, who are not less considerable than the others, are truly merchants, that is to say, such as receive commissions from abroad to buy cloth for the merchants chiefly in Hamburg, and in Holland, and several other parts.
>
> These are not only many in number, but some of them are very

considerable in their dealings, and correspond as far as Nuremberg, Frankfurt, Leipzig, and even to Vienna and Augsburg, in the farthest provinces of Germany.

In the ten years between 1732 and 1741, it was recorded (at the Easter Quarter Sessions, held at Pontefract) that 'Yorkshire' manufactured and sold 580,646 pieces. In the following ten years there were 1,236,304 and in the ten years ending in 1771 the number had grown to 1,546,823. By 1821 the ten-year figure (the decade that included the Napoleonic wars) had grown to 4.5million.

The largest area of the Yorkshire wool production region, taking in Ilkley, Keighley, Bingley, Shipley, Haworth, Bradford, Morley, Cleckheaton, and across to Wakefield wove and sold mostly white cloth. A near north-south strip within in it, from Otley, via Guiseley, Rawdon, Horsforth, Bramley, Armley Leeds, Pudsey, Hensley, Dewsbury, Ossett and Mirfield made both coloured and white. Halifax, Sowerby Bridge and Elland specialised in kerseys. The small area that included Batley, Dewsbury, Ossett and Heckmondwike became the actual 'Heavy Woollen District'.

Transporting all this wool could not have been easy. First, the 'woolpack' of fleeces, although light in weight, was usually large and, because the containers were often soaked in the grease (natural lanolin) they were difficult to handle, so stones were sewn into the corners to make them easier to lift. These 'ears' are visible on artists' illustrations of woolpacks, which are frequently depicted, where appropriate, in local coats of arms and pub signs.

Then the wool, often big quantities of it, needed to be moved from the halls either for finishing or to be despatched around the country, for sale or for tailoring or for export, producing yet more work for carters.

The Worsted Revolution

It would appear likely – if not self-evident – that the manufacture of 'worsted' had started in Yorkshire at least as early as it had in East Anglia, but that it had been overtaken by the production of cheap kerseys and northern dozens. It was not until around 1700 that West Riding manufacturers made a serious foray into the production of shalloons and tammies (a mixture or worsted and cotton).

Other towns, scattered across the country, had their specialities: Exeter was also famous for its serges, Canterbury and Colchester were known to make good sayes, Coventry was producing tammies, and so on. But they were all small beer.

Yorkshire's progress may have been slow, but there was no stopping it. It was an industrial revolution that would take the best part of a century to reach fruition.

It has been estimated that in 1700 Yorkshire's share of the wool industry output was only about one–fifth; by 1770 it was about one–third, and the Riding reigned supreme in all matters concerning wool. By 1800 it had increased its share of production to around three–fifths.

Quite how it had happened is still a subject for conjecture. Some say that the weavers of East Anglia shifted to the north to avoid restrictions and regulations that had been specifically applied to Norfolk; or that East Anglian weavers relocated because both land and labour were cheaper in the north, or that, having dithered for so long while Lancashire introduced successful factory working for cotton the West Riding was the first region to react by trying to copy it, or that the weavers themselves decided to up their game in order to relieve widespread poverty in the area. Or it may be that all of them were contributory factors.

Meanwhile, Norfolk had been aiding its own demise by putting out wool for spinning in Yorkshire for the manufacture of its own textiles, thus increasing the power and extending the influence of the West Riding in the industry. Perhaps, then, it made more sense to have all the business conducted in one place.

Around the same time the industry's stake holders in Yorkshire – the big farmers, the weavers, the clothiers and the merchants – had been searching for a change in direction.

Foreign manufacturers had started making their own cheap clothes and were introducing low prices and thereby undercutting the English product.

In 1670 a writer in Lille wrote that:

> 'The French are now got into a way of making a low-price sort of cloath called Searge de Berry which comes as cheap as Northern cloaths and of much better wool... in which they have cloathed a great number of their soldiers'.

The projections for the future of kerseys and other cheap textiles did not appear bright. One solution seemed to be to switch from cheap and rough cloths to fine and more expensive textiles for which there was a thriving market.

The change occurred as the 17th century merged with the 18th. This – the late Stuart period – is the time worsteds became inextricably bound with the areas around Bradford and Halifax (but mainly around and in Halifax).

The introductory stage was the creation of 'bays', half woollen, half worsted (the warp being combed, the weft being carded). In 1706, one of the first big traders, Joseph Holroyd of Halifax, regularly bought 40 pieces at a time for selling in London and overseas, as well as at least one consignment of 250 pieces to ship to a single customer in Rotterdam.

'Full' worsteds had not yet come to the fore, but there are records of serges and shalloons starting to replace the local 'dozens'. Wool–combers were prolific in Leeds around 1710. The Skipton parish register records wool–combers in 1717 while Keighley's notes a shalloon maker in 1724 and a woolcomb maker the following year.

Keighley was regularly sending shalloon pieces to London at this time while Denholme and Haworth became early and flourishing centres of actual 'worsted'.

By 1750 the Riding had extended its expertise to the manufacture of calamanco, a thin fabric of worsted wool yarn which could come in a variety of weaves: plain, satin, damasked, or brocaded in floral, striped and checked designs. The surface was glazed or calendared (pressed through hot rollers) or by rubbing with a stone or by applying hot wax to the surface.

It also pressed on with shalloons and tammies in an area centred, for both woollens and worsteds, around

Halifax and spread as far as Wakefield and Leeds (which was basically a finishing and dyeing, as well as a trading centre, with a population of maybe 6,000).

Halifax (population about 10,000) had nevertheless not turned its back on the manufacture of kerseys. The demand for uniform cloths for troops in the various wars of the 18th century would guarantee a steady trade for the town which meanwhile was also producing an estimated 100,000 shalloon pieces every year for export to Spain, Portugal, Italy and the Levant, in addition to home consumption.

The colossal Halifax Piece Hall served weavers from the industrious parish itself, as well as from Keighley, Haworth and Colne, and merchants from Leeds would buy white cloth there for exporting, unfinished, to Holland and Hamburg.

The very presence of the Piece Hall had attracted worsted weavers, clothiers and merchants to move into the town and supported the trade of inns with lodgings and refreshment for visitors. Its heyday was to be the Regency period under Georges III and IV.

Right at the end of that Georgian era the sons of John Crossley, who ran a small water-powered spinning mill, moved into carpet making. Their Dean Clough mills became the major local employer, and eventually the biggest carpet factory in the world.

Wakefield, in the 18th century a close second to Halifax in its importance as a worsted centre, also experienced great prosperity, its success enhanced by the production of a new type of tammies, glazed and sold at home and abroad for window blinds and curtains. The opening of the Aire and Calder Navigation had meant that long-haired wool from Lincolnshire and Leicestershire – the perfect wool for worsted weaving – could be brought by boat to be sold in Wakefield market in its raw state.

Wakefield then became the centre for all worsted trading, whether in its raw or woven state. At the same time it gained a reputation for dressing and finishing cloths from elsewhere: in direct competition with Leeds (which was concentrating on woollens). Warehouses had to be built to cope with the amount of product being bought and sold within the town. Wakefield was considered a fine town with clean streets: the River Calder was so clear that it was said that salmon were seen leaping the dam wall at Kirkgate.

Statistics from the 18th century can rarely be assumed to be accurate, being often based on estimates mingled with a few facts and sometimes with a host of suppositions. Nevertheless, a Parliamentary Committee reported the Output of Worsteds For The West Riding in 1772 as being £1,404,000.

The world of worsted was therefore going on around Bradford, but not in it. It remained a small town of little significance, with a market, a couple of small mills and a population in 1780 of about 4,200. (By 1800 it would be 13,600.)

Cloth sold 'in the white' at its market or Piece Hall went directly to Leeds for finishing, dyeing and for ultimately exporting. Leeds was also where the majority of merchants lived and where there were offices for the tradesmen and inns for visitors.

The years of the West Riding's ascendancy had coincided dramatically with the period of the Anglo–Dutch Wars, the four 17th and 18th century English naval conflicts with the Dutch Republic. The first three wars would establish England's naval might, and the last, arising from Dutch interference in the American Revolution, spelled the end of the Holland's position as a world power.

The wars were about commerce, and commerce was chiefly about wool. Since Charles II had banned the export of wool, England was (officially) trading only finished cloths. But the Dutch – if they could not get the actual wool to feed their own looms – at least wanted raw cloths for their own large community of finishers and dyers who, even the English conceded, were superior in those skills.

Most European countries had started to recognise the need for self-sufficiency, including making their own cloth and clothing themselves and their armies. But to achieve that situation they needed wool, and fullers' earth, and they had only scant supplies of both.

> 'Wool is the flower and strength, the revenue and blood of England and in the supply of fullers' earth this nation is by God peculiarised in these blessings... It is possible and probable that other parts of the world may produce Fullers' earth, but neither in such fineness nor abundance as this in England.'

So wrote the author of *The Golden Fleece*, known only as 'W S (Gentleman)', in 1656.

But there was no embargo on the exporting of looms or other wool making equipment. Nor, until 1718, was there any law against exporting wool makers.

In October 1727 two cloth-dressers, John Windsor and William Simpson, were accused at the Leeds General Sessions of having

> 'promised and contracted to leave the realm of Great Britain and go to Spain, there to exercise their art and to teach the mystery of cloth-dressing to the subjects of the King of Spain'.

The prosecution, however, broke down, and the men were acquitted.

Nevertheless, when Prussia and Russia wanted to create their own textile industries they sought out English experts who could set up and instruct their people in the art of wool cloth making. There are many reports of this kind of practice succeeding, including one, in 1738, in a pamphlet titled *Observations on British wool and the Manufacture of it*, which identifies a Mr John Hudson of Yorkshire who travelled to Alton (in the city state of Hamburg) and had been making cloth there for six years.

> 'And now there is at that place above 100 looms and those that are gone over lately are to set up the making of stuffs and stockings and narrow goods and have carried their engines and other utensils along with them and several broad looms to make calamancos, camblets and divers other stuffs.'

But there would be light at the end of the tunnel.

The first glimmer was the development of Britain's commercial and colonial empire, the foundations of which had been fully cast during the previous century. India, North America, and other territories opened up sources of new material or provided new markets, and a brisk trade in cloth soon developed between Yorkshire and the North American colonies. At the same time the European market was extended by an old treaty which opened Portugal still further to English cloth dealers, and by the relations of William of Orange and the Hanoverian kings across Europe. As the English navy gained greater mastery over the sea the complaints of piracy or harassment became less frequent, and merchants could make their journeys or ship their products in peace and security.

Meanwhile, on the home front, economic activity was developed during the last decade of the 1600s: the founding of the Bank of England, the institution of the National Debt, the restoration of the currency, and the developments in credit, paper money, and marine insurance, all helped British commerce to grow towards a state of greater efficiency and more complex organisation. The commercial class grew in wealth and importance, and although the old pioneer companies had lost their former influence, newer associations, such as the East India Company, had achieved more political and economic power over the regions in which they traded.

Yorkshire's merchants and financiers decided to extend their influence on parliament by standing as candidates and that way achieved status with assumed respectability.

Defoe may have been the first to recognise the shift in status:

> 'Trade is so far from being inconsistent with a gentleman that in England trade makes a gentleman, for after a generation or two, the tradesman's children come to be as good gentlemen, statesmen, parliament-men, judges, bishops and noblemen as those of the highest birth and most ancient families.'
>
> (*The Complete English Tradesman*, 1727)

The nobility itself was helpful, at least in Yorkshire,

where the first Piece Hall was built for the weavers of Halifax by Viscount Irwin in 1708 and the first White Cloth Hall by him in Leeds in 1711.

The gentry and nobility of the county supported the creation of turnpike and canal ventures creating better facilities for the purchase of land for better roads or for making rivers navigable, thus facilitating the movement of all industrial products.

By the second half of the 18th century most of the population's sartorial taste had shifted enthusiastically towards worsteds.

Merchants appeared everywhere, riding out from Leeds through town to town and valley to valley, buying up the pieces, many of them for sale to the continent.

Weaving became the primary occupation for most men, although those who were concerned with caring for sheep sometimes counted the two jobs equally. Within a short time, by splitting their efforts between shepherding and domestic weaving, Yorkshire farmers with their naturally thrifty habits, were able to purchase their homestead and farm.

Everybody, it appeared, wanted a part of the new worsted trade – some of them sorting, some fulling, some weaving, and spinning began to be taught to girls at school.

Although worsted had been woven in Yorkshire for years, a new era had begun.

By the end of the 18th century cotton, imported from the American colonies and finding a friendly climate had displaced wool production in Lancashire, leaving the field wide open to Yorkshire. And while the north–west was fully transforming its industry, the wool men of Yorkshire received new vigour from all that was happening around them and began the development of the West Riding along dual lines, as a woollen and also as a worsted manufacturing county.

It was not until the very turn of the century, when it combined its birthright of coal, iron and water into steam power and machinery that Bradford's progress began to take shape.

In 1773 it had opened a Piece Hall replacing the White Lion pub as its marketplace for wool, where weavers could rent, or share, one of 300 spaces or could set up stalls in a central hall to sell both finished and unfinished worsted pieces every Thursday, and later, as production increased, also on Mondays. Regular weavers had their own lockable cupboards where they could leave their unsold pieces until the following week's sale.

But, still, Bradford was a cloth–market, rather than a cloth–weaving, town.

The weaving was being done in 'Bradford-dale', but not in the town itself.

The following year a link to the Leeds and Liverpool Canal had given the town much greater accessibility. Lying as it was in the eastern foothills of the Pennines, with direct links to Leeds and Halifax – and ultimately to Liverpool in one direction and Hull in the other – it seemed ideally placed, not only for the West Riding but for the rest of England.

And the opening of a railway line from Leeds in 1854 would give the town even greater access. Halifax could now be reached by rail only via Bradford, so its supreme importance was diminished.

Bradford was set to become the new metropolis for worsteds: *'Worstedopolis'*, some called it (reportedly).

But Leeds was still the heart and home of the wool industry. It was making a cloth called 'camblet'. A rough, thick, worsted material, it was considered especially valuable for resisting wind and rain and was therefore useful in the making of cloaks and wraps for people travelling by coach. The cloth would remain popular until the advent of railway travelling and, with it, the invention of the light raincoat – at which time Leeds started weaving material for light raincoats. This led to the creation of the iconic Burberry trenchcoat and to branded raincoats manufactured in Leeds, Castleford and Keighley.

Bradford was ready, willing and able to compete and with the combination of such determined towns as its strongholds, the worsted industry grew steadily around it throughout the century. The West Riding had experienced years of bad trade and of good, had lost old markets and gained new ones. But it would gradually win from southerly manufacturers the monopoly or predominance which they had formerly enjoyed. The tammies of Wakefield replaced those of Coventry, the serges of Exeter fought in vain against the growing popularity of Halifax and, now, of Bradford cloth. And Norfolk, instead of paying Yorkshire spinners to feed its looms, started to send the yarn spun in its own homes.

Transport

Second only to the sheep, in the early history of the wool industry, the most important animal was the horse.

Distances were (or would appear to be) so great that it is reasonable to assume that the shearer would journey with his necessary equipment on horseback. In the sequence of the trade, the horse would appear, next, as a pack animal, probably as part of a train, with the travelling pedlar or merchant who relieved the shepherd of his fleeces, or of his pieces, or of both. The horse-train would create and then follow meandering 'bridle paths', alongside river-beds or on the crests of hills and moors between the remote cottages and villages, heading for market towns where the wares could be sorted and sold. These paths would eventually link the east coast at Hull to the west coast at Liverpool with deviations in between, although there would soon be more conventional 'roads' between the major towns such as Hull, York, Leeds, Wakefield and Halifax, as well as cart tracks made by the carriage of coal from the Bradford area to industrial and residential centres in both Yorkshire and Lancashire.

Next – especially as the wool product progressed from fleeces to pieces – came the horse-and-cart. Every village had its carter: it was at first a job description and then, consequently, became a surname. Larger villages had more than one. They would publish their times for departure to the cloth halls and if the 'maister' or weaver was not ready with his pieces for market, the carter stuck to his timetable and left without them. From, say, Farsley, to the centre of Leeds might take about an hour; the important requirement was that he arrived at the market before it opened, otherwise deals may be missed.

In 1811, Abimelech Hainsworth, founder of the textile dynasty that survives today, kept four pack horses at the Cape of Good Hope mill on the Bramley side of the Bagley beck (which separates Farsley township from Bramley) to take his coloured cloth for sale in Leeds, twice a week.

But most smaller producers relied on carters, either to take their goods to Leeds or, once the canal was available, to loading docks maybe a mile away at Rodley Basin, and onto barges that would be met at Wellington Bridge by more carters who would convey the finished pieces a short distance to the halls.

Then there were the horse-drawn carriages that conveyed the 'maisters' to market in order for them to be on site to oversee the sale of their pieces – and often to buy wool (to be taken back in bales by the local carter) to keep the looms in steady employment.

There would be more carts to take the finished wool pieces for sale to tailors in the rest of Yorkshire, and beyond, as well as to Hull, for exporting.

When steam power – even when it was used only (with a totally incomprehensible mechanical naivety) to keep waterwheels turning – was introduced, draught horses pulled the coal carts to the mills.

There were so many horses and horses–and–carts that traffic congestion in urban areas was inevitable, although there was no clip–clopping of passing traffic to be heard, as their iron hooves trod mostly on increasing levels of their own droppings, which remained unswept and uncollected.

Although it was believed that Romans drove and marched 'on the left' and in 1300AD Pope Boniface VIII had declared that all pilgrims travelling to Rome should keep to the left, there were no 'rules of the road' until the Highway Act of 1835 which introduced a 'Keep Left' law for carriages throughout the British Empire.

In the villages, drays delivered barrels of beer to the pubs, and then horse–drawn carts arrived to collect the by–product of the breweries… the 'stale' urine that was used for bleaching and for fixing dyes. Referred to in polite circles as 'old wash' it was decanted into vast tubs at the mills, downwind and out of the sun – an ancient form of recycling.

This part of the process obviously involved cartmen visiting a number of pubs and inns to make their collections. And the temptation to tarry in some of them must have been great, for in 1839 the mill owners decreed that any carrier calling at a public house except on business during working hours would be dismissed.

The last use of 'old wash' in the first and final processes of wool passed without being recorded, but it was certainly still in use during the 1850s, when it started to be replaced by ammonia.

And finally came the stagecoaches on which the rich merchants would sometimes embark for London both to arrange deals with foreign buyers or even to buy fine wool from the other counties, or to visit their agents who sold the finished worsteds to London tailors.

They allowed four days for the journey ('God willing' said some of the timetables) – with three overnight stops at coaching inns – stopping every 15 or so miles in order to refresh the four horses and cost about £2 (or a penny per mile) in the 1700s. Leeds became a hub for mail coaches, providing postal connections with Halifax, Huddersfield and York, journeying via Sheffield, Nottingham, Melton Mowbray, Kettering, Bedford and Barnet three days a week. Four passengers were allowed inside, and three or four on top, beside an armed guard.

The coaches often also carried mail between the

towns. Stagecoaches travelled along turnpikes (toll roads), the guard on a mail coach blowing a post-horn to signal its approach and open the gates to allow free passage for the Royal Mail.

The busiest roads obviously became deeply rutted by iron-wheeled traffic and could be near-unusable in bad weather, and beyond the ability of parishes (whose responsibility it was) to maintain. So stretches of main roads were leased to groups of businessmen (or to 'turnpike trusts') who would keep them in good repair, and impose a charge, in the form of a toll for their use.

Within the West Riding there were, for example, turnpikes between

> Leeds and Birstall, Collingham, Halifax, Harrogate, Hebden Bridge, Holmfield Lane End, Otley, Roundhay, Selby, Tong Lane End, Wakefield, Whitehall, Sheffield, and Woodhouse Carr...
> Between Bradford and Eccleshill, Huddersfield, Thornton, Wakefield, Colne, and Heckmondwike...
> Between Halifax and Huddersfield, Sheffield, Dewsbury, and Littleborough...
> Between Wakefield and Aberford, Austerlands, Denby Dale, Halifax, Sheffield, Weeland, and Pontefract...

And maybe about 100 more.

The Leeds-Bradford-Halifax road was 'turnpiked' in 1740.

Toll charges varied greatly: in some cases 10 pence per draught horse, in others, one penny per pair of wheels, in others, two shillings a coach. Some turnpikes charged according to the width of iron tyres (narrow tyres causing most damage to road surfaces).

Sheep were charged by the score, but were allowed

to pass freely when being moved to fresh pastures.

Some colliers made advance agreements (around £50 a year) for their coal wagons to use the turnpikes regularly.

Not surprisingly, attempts were sometimes made to evade or reduce toll charges. In 1775 the *Leeds Intelligencer* recorded that:

> On Tuesday last a farmer at Allerton Grange, near this town was convicted in the penalty of four pounds... for taking of two of his horses from the cart, in order to evade turnpike tolls.

Turnpikes would fade out with the coming of the railways.

But, first, had come the canals...

Canals and Coaches

The Romans (of course) had introduced man–made waterways to Britain. Although primarily intended for drainage, it is uncertain to what, if to any, extent they were also used for transport. Without doubt some of the channels they dug out were wide enough and sufficiently deep to have handled some form of water navigation.

Following the departure of the Romans the canals fell into disrepair until the middle ages when some, such as the Foss Dyke, first built around 120AD to connect Lincoln to the River Trent, were restored, and waterways providing both drainage and navigability were created, in order to ease passages on the rivers Idle, Hull, Don and Ouse.

An Act signed in 1462 by Edward IV ordered the dredging of the Ouse to make it navigable to (Kingston upon) Hull – which had been founded by monks in the 12th century as Wyke on Hull (Wyke meaning 'outlying settlement') as a port from which to export their wool. It was renamed as 'King's Town upon Hull' in 1299.

Water transport was thereby introduced to convey vital supplies of grain – and, later, of coal – from the north of England to the south, while also greatly assisting the movement of wool for export.

In the early 1600s the River Aire was navigable for boats carrying up to 30 tons as far as Knottingley, and for most of the century the merchants of Leeds were proposing links to the river while representatives from York were opposing it (rightly, as it happens) on the basis that greater access for Leeds would diminish the importance of the Ouse, and thence of the domination of York as a commercial centre.

The Aire and Calder Navigation Act was finally passed in 1699 and within five years the Aire was navigable to Leeds and the Calder as far as Wakefield.

Landowners, by now learning much more about agricultural sustainability, fertilisation, irrigation and land drainage, generally supported the projects, seeing navigation as being only incidentally useful, as a means of conveying coal and lime (as a fertiliser) to their farms, and for getting their produce to market.

The route of the canal bypassed Bradford, but a link from the town centre to meet it at Shipley was opened in 1774. Initially used for the transport of stone and coal, in 1828 a passenger service was introduced to carry people between Bradford and Leeds.

Meanwhile the Leeds merchants were increasing their access westwards towards Liverpool – known as 'the second city of the British Empire' – to service their wool exports to America (and to the rest of the world beyond Europe) with the creation of the Leeds and Liverpool Canal which would be opened along its 127 miles distance across the Pennine hills in 1816. The first passage through it departed from Leeds on October 19 and passed Wigan three days later. But for passengers, horse drawn transport was much faster and was therefore the preferred form of transport.

LOOK HERE!

A NEW COACH
FROM BRADFORD TO MANCHESTER,
IN THREE HOURS AND A HALF CERTAIN!!

FROM the earnest solicitations which have been made, the undermentioned Proprietors are now induced to put on a New Light Post Safety Coach, called the *Hirondelle*, which commenced Running on MONDAY the Third instant, and will leave the Bowling Green Inn, at a Quarter past Three P.M., passing through Huddersfield, Marsden, Delph, and Oldham, and arrive in Manchester, in time for the Liverpool, Preston, and Birmingham Trains; and will return through the above mentioned Towns, leaving the Angel and Royal Hotel Offices, Manchester, at a Quarter past Nine A.M.

The Proprietors of the above Coach beg to state that it will be conducted in a style not to be surpassed, and will be driven by that well known Coachman JERRY SCOTT, for many years Coachman on the Leeds Road.

Performed by the Public's obedient Servants,
T. BRADFORD, & Co.,
H. TOWLER,
J. BUCKLEY, & SON, and
J. GREENWOOD.

N. B. By request, and for the special accommodation of the Merchants and Gentlemen attending the Bradford Market, the time of starting from the Two Places will be altered as under, for THURSDAYS ONLY, viz.:—

From MANCHESTER at Seven A.M.
From BRADFORD at 5 P.M.
And on every other Day of the Week as before stated.
Bradford, June 31st, 1843.

From conception to completion the Canal had taken 76 years to achieve its original purpose – built in sections to link the North Sea to the Irish Sea and thereby create access in both directions for exports. By 1843 steam power had been introduced to create the first tugboats.

Without their realising it, the influence and power of the landed classes was diminishing as the importance of the north of England merchant class had grown.

It had taken a long time for Yorkshire's population to appreciate that in its south-west it possessed, beyond any doubt, more natural advantages for manufacturing than anywhere else in the kingdom, having (in abundance) fast–flowing water, coal, and ironstone. That is of course in addition to being surrounded by sheep.

With all its small valleys, its rills, brooks and rivers could be adapted either for the use of waterpower, driving waterwheels, or for feeding, along with coal, 'that great iron servant of nations', the steam engine.

The West Yorkshire coalfield stretched to Derby and Nottingham, one of the most valuable and productive and most easily worked in the country. Iron was found at the very doorstep of the machine-maker and the machine-user.

Add to this the fact of it being centrally placed, and populated by an industrious tribe of people with energy for both labour and trade, and it becomes easy to understand how the West Riding became the principal seat of industry once England started to develop.

Industrial Revelation

Any industrial revolution – if one translates it as innovation and discards its meaning of popular revolt – involves no more than the introduction of significant modern production methods. But 'modern' relates to the time.

Hence, the spinning wheel replacing the distaff (probably in England during the 15th century) must have been revolutionary and the treadle–powered wheel more revolutionary still, because the spinner could now work the wool with both hands.

What was once modern and innovative would become ancient soon afterwards, especially if it had been replaced by a new (more 'modern') product.

The gradual replacement of the ubiquitous and well-tried distaff in shepherds' homes would have increased the speed of thread making by more than ten times – it nevertheless remained precision work, slow in comparison with the swiftness of work at the loom.

James Hargreaves' 'spinning jenny' (1764), a machine that, by turning a wheel (by hand) could spin a large number of spindles at the same time, was certainly revolutionary. Until its invention it had required at least five spinners to satisfy the needs of one working weaver.

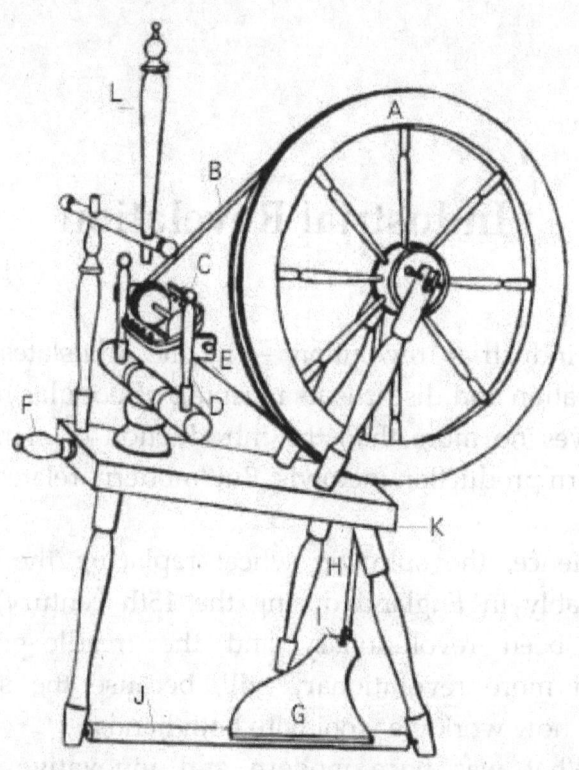

Parts of a treadle wheel: A – Wheel, B – Drive band, C – Flyer assembly, D – Maiden, E – Bearings, F – Tension Screw, G – Treadle, H – Footman, I – Treadle connection, J – Treadle bar, K – Table, L – Distaff

Fifty years later there would be hardly any hand-spinning in the Riding as machinery took over. Labour costs dropped and production soared.

John Kay, born in Bury, was apprenticed as a hand-loom reed maker (the reed was a device, like a comb, that separated and spaced the warp threads, guided the shuttle's motion across the loom, and gently pushed the weft threads together), but after a month he quit his apprenticeship, claiming to have mastered the business.

He invented a metal substitute for the natural reed and patented a cording and twisting machine for worsted.

In 1733 he patented his most revolutionary device: something he called a 'wheeled shuttle', that accelerated weaving by allowing the shuttle carrying the weft to be passed back and forth through the warp threads faster and over a greater width of cloth because the weaver did not need to pass the shuttle back with his other hand: the machine itself did that. The device moved so quickly across the loom that it soon became known as the 'flying shuttle'.

Kay's invention put the shuttle on wheels and controlled it with a driver, attached to a cord. Pull the cord to the right and the shuttle shot (or 'flew') the weft across and under and over the warp; pull it to the left and the shuttle came back in a similar way.

The Flying Shuttle, needing nobody at the other side to send the weft back was therefore able to do the work of two people producing broadcloth (which could be as wide as nine feet), and at a greater speed. Kay's problem, however, was that once one machine had been acquired it was easily copied. He had a patent, but the weavers did not want to pay him for it, they even formed an association to fight his legal claim for royalties.

Kay lost all of his money in legal battles to defend his patent and it is believed that he eventually moved to France where he died a poor man.

With pedal-powered spinning wheels and looms with flying shuttles, wool production appeared to have gone about as far as it could go. Domestic weaving remained the norm but the scale and speed had become industrial.

Such revolutionary inventions made life easier for the spinners and weavers: so nobody complained about their involving less work.

Revolution

The Industrial Revolution, as we recall it, started most visibly in the textile industry in Lancashire around the mid-1700s and continued throughout the century and well into the next one as manufacturers of both wool and cotton strived to find more efficient ways of both spinning and weaving. But the wool industry was not, by a long chalk, a major factor of this so-called 'revolution'.

There were so many significant inventions and changes in industry that professional historians are unable to agree when it started or when it ended – or even whether, in fact, it ever ended. Indeed, some of them now refer to the innovative changes towards the end of the 18th century as only the 'first' industrial revolution.

The revolution is inevitably associated with the advent of steam power, an invention that changed the face and the structure of industries, especially of textile and coal and iron production. (Coal was used to drive iron steam engines that pumped water out of the mines so that more coal could be produced to power the iron machines for industries that were now relying on steam.). The first (water–) powered textile mill had been built (for silk) in Derbyshire in 1717, but Richard

Arkwright's cotton–spinning mills in the 1770s became the archetype of the early modern factory with a layout planned to facilitate a near-continuous flow of materials through one building.

Steam–powered looms (being invented about the same time as powered spinning and introduced cautiously into the cotton industry) worked on the same basic process as man–operated looms, but replaced the pedal–power source needed to draw the weft threads through the warp, also reducing the skill (and the number of operators) required to weave the cloth. Steam power would also produce a consistent quality of weaving.

By the turn of the century Lancastrian cotton mills had adapted steam power for both spinning and weaving, thereby creating what would become known as 'vertical mills' – with raw materials coming in one door and finished textiles going out of another.

On the eastern slopes of the Pennines there were around 80 textile mills boasting steam power, but contemporary reports and insurance records show that, in Yorkshire, rather than using the steam engine's own wheel to turn a wheel – or even to turn the water wheel itself – the machine was being used to pump water back upstream, to flow back down again.

An advertisement in the *Leeds Intelligencer* in April 1799 described

> A newly erected Water Fulling and Scribbling Mill situate upon Farnley Beck, within the township of Farnley, with a steam engine for throwing back the water upon the wheel when necessary.

Yorkshire's clothiers were remarkably slow to take

full advantage of the new technology. Spinning did not become a factory industry until 1794 in Bradford, provoking a small riot which came to nought, but elsewhere not generally applied until around 1820, and a substantial amount of woollen yarn was still being spun in spinsters' own homes. Powered weaving of wool progressed even more slowly, on the grounds that, because of its elasticity and crimp, and lower tensile strength, it was less easy to weave wool than cotton in a machine.

When wool was mixed with silk, or cotton, there was a difference in tensile strength; alpaca fleeces had a different style of crimp; silk was vegetable matter, goats had hair, not fleeces. It took time to sort out the different degrees of pressure required for production of any wool mixtures, but by trial and error the mill-owners found ways to do it, starting eventually with the production of pure wool cloth.

The first powered weaving was seen in Bradford in the mid-1820s (weaving cotton mixed with wool), but handloom weaving of wool would remain common well into the 19th century – in some cases until the 1880s.

On that basis, the West Riding might be considered to have watched the industrial revolution pass it by.

There had, in fact, been one – only one – bold, not to say reckless, early attempt to introduce powered weaving east of the Pennines.

The first feasible power loom had been invented by Edmund Cartwright in 1785, and although it was initially a fairly crude device it established the basic principle and, being continuously improved, would be used in the industry until the 20th century. Three years later his elder brother John opened Revolution Mill, which was powered, according to the original device, by a Boulton and Watt steam engine and had 108 power looms on three floors as well as steam–powered spinning machinery.

[The mill was not named for the 'industrial revolution', but because it was opened in the centenary year of the 'Glorious Revolution' when William of Orange and his supporters deposed King James II.]

Although no trace of it has survived, some usually authoritative sources locate the site of the mill in Doncaster – which would, at least, have placed it in the proximity of a Yorkshire coalfield. But it was actually about 15 miles away – too great a distance and too high a cost for the haulage of coal by horse–drawn wagon –

on a ten-acre site on Spital Hill at Clarborough in East Retford, Nottinghamshire, where John Cartwright intended to stand for parliament.

His only previous employment had been in the Royal Marines, where he achieved the rank of major. He knew nothing about wool or weaving and had no experience of machinery, industry or commerce. He had not taken into account the cost of buying and installing so many looms. Far from replacing jobs, his mill needed a staff of 600 master weavers, which was impossible to find among the local population of East Retford. Within two years the mill had failed, was put into the hands of its creditors, and offered for sale.

An advertisement in the *Leeds Intelligencer* gives some idea of its ambitious scale. In addition to the extensive estate was

> 'a large, commodious and well-built spinning mill... with out-buildings of great magnitude and extent, containing every conveniency properly appendant to a spinning mill and on an ample scale: such as wool-room, washing houses, drying houses, warehouses and accommodation for children; also 19 dwelling houses, besides stables and workshops of every denomination.'

There was 'a capital steam engine', plus 'machinery of every necessary sort, for combing, drawing, roving, spinning and other operations upon wool...'

Before the auction took place the power looms had been sold on... to a cotton factory in Lancashire.

History teaches us, as an equally important and inseparably linked factor of the industrial revolution, that the 'Luddite' movement was totally opposed to changes in industrial processes. Even today we use that term, Luddite, to describe a person who is opposed to any form of new technology. The Luddites, however, insisted that they were not opposed to machinery, *per se*, but to the unemployment it created. They said they were fighting, not against innovation and invention (with which many of them already worked), but in favour of 'the commonality', i.e. for the common good. They said they wanted real jobs with apprenticeships, and more jobs with higher rates of pay, but men with jobs had to have priority against machines that might replace them and take away their livelihood.

Luddites

The Luddite movement considered itself a secret society on the simple but obviously flawed basis that, if its members did not know the identities of their comrades, they could never be forced to betray them. Reportedly, they covered their faces with scarves at meetings and during military–style training activities. They were led (at least, in theory) by 'General Ludd', a fictional character living, like Robin Hood, in Sherwood Forest, and may have been named after a genuine person called Ned (Edward) Ludlum or Ludlam or perhaps Ludnam or even Ludd. He was (supposedly) an apprentice who reportedly and 'famously' broke two Nottinghamshire stocking-making machines in 'a fit of passion'. There appear, however, to be no local birth or baptism records for anybody with that name, or approximate name and likely age, and there are certainly no records of anybody with that name being arrested. And yet it somehow became commonplace; when asking who had broken any machinery, the response would often be 'Ned Ludd'.

'General Ludd' first appeared (*in absentia*) during a protest about machines replacing men in Nottingham in March 1811. Troops were called in to break up the crowd and this may have been what prompted the idea

of a need for a Luddite 'army'. Its elusive leader clearly inspired the protesters and very soon stories of his apparent command of unseen armies, often drilling by moonlight, caused all government agencies to make his arrest their primary goal.

But the Luddites were neither as organised nor as dangerous, either as they pretended or as authorities believed. They set some factories and mills on fire, but mainly they confined themselves to breaking machines. And in the event they suffered more injuries than they inflicted.

Immediately after the first protest, attacks occurred almost nightly, but then sporadically and afterwards in military waves, spreading eventually as guerrilla warfare into Lancashire and the Yorkshire borders. In Lancashire the Luddites were fighting the introduction of steam–powered looms in the cotton industry, which were undercutting the cloth production by handloom weavers, who still largely worked in their own cottages. In Yorkshire, the new technology involved nothing newer than water power.

However, the Luddite movement provides some sort of fixed dating for the 'industrial revolution'.

Fearing what appeared to be a popular uprising, the government posted thousands of troops – more in total than Wellington had to fight against Napoleon – around the northern mills and factories. There were 1,000 troops in Huddersfield alone. A law, the Frame Breaking Act, which made industrial sabotage a capital offence, was passed in 1812.

The truth was that the Luddites did attract a lot of public support. At the start of the 19th century northerners in the various woollen trades had been comfortably engaged, and mostly self-employed. But wars with France, Prussia and America had created economic confusion. Apart from those mills working for the army, with exports impossible to both east and west, textile workers started to experience what one historian described as 'the hard pinch of poverty, where it had hitherto been a stranger'.

Subsisting at near starvation level, the West Riding clothiers had very little work, and the work that was on offer was poorly paid. Some weaving continued in the recession nevertheless, and the last part of the production process was the cloth-shearing or cropping, to improve the appearance of the saleable wool. This work had started to be put out to professional 'cropping sheds'. Where there was woven wool, even in meagre amounts, there was work for croppers.

But some progressive mill owners had started to introduce water-driven cropping machines which worked much faster but just as efficiently as the shearers that they had employed. The skilled and diligent – and highly paid – cloth shearers were quickly becoming redundant (in an age that had no concept of relief as 'redundancy pay') and were being replaced by low-paid and unskilled machine minders.

Cropping machine

One night early in April 1812 the local Luddites lay in wait on Hartshead Moor and ambushed wagons carrying new cropping frames. The drivers were taken prisoner and held until all the machinery had been smashed with sledgehammers that they called 'Enochs' – because they were made by a company in Marsden owned by Enoch Taylor and which, perhaps ironically, had also manufactured the cropping frames.

'Enoch hath made 'em and Enochs shall break 'em,' became a slogan of the Luddite gangs.

On April 9 they made a massive attack on Foster's Mill at Horbury again taking their 'Enochs' to the cropping frames.

Flushed with success, some 150 Luddites, led by a young Huddersfield cropper called George Mellor, met in Mirfield and set out to Rawfolds Mill near Cleckheaton the following Saturday night, April 11.

William Cartwright, the acting owner of the mill (at this time he was still trying to raise the necessary money to buy it) had installed water-powered cropping frames, with which, for a fee, he put the final touches to other people's weaving.

The attackers wore masks or blackened their faces and were armed with some pistols, but mostly old swords or home-made weapons. They were joined by Luddites from Leeds and were nearly 300 strong by the time they reached the mill...

Rawfolds Mill

Under the headlines RIOTS AND FATAL CONFLICT, this is how the attack was investigated and reported in the *Leeds Mercury* on Saturday, April 18:

> We have made it our business to collect a faithful narrative of the sanguinary contest that last Saturday night took place at Rawfolds, between the men calling themselves the army of General Ludd and the persons employed in guarding the property of Mr Cartwright, in order to place upon record the particulars of an event that will survive in local remembrance the present generation; and we can undertake to say, that the following narrative may be implicitly relied upon:
>
> It is known to our readers that the use of machinery for raising

and dressing woollen cloth has of late become very unpopular amongst the shearmen in this part of the country; and that all mills where machinery of this kind is in use have been marked out for destruction and that in several of them the obnoxious machines have been destroyed.

At Rawfolds, near Cleckheaton, a place at an equal distance from Huddersfield and Leeds, from each of which it is about eight miles, a gentleman of the name of William Cartwright has a mill used for the purpose of dressing cloth in the way objected to by the men; on this mill it was understood that an attempt was to be made; and on Thursday night, the 9th inst. the sentinel at the mill observed several signals that were supposed to indicate an approaching attack, though both that and the following night passed over without molestation.

On Saturday night, about half–past twelve, there was a firing heard from the north which was answered from the south, and again from west to east; this firing was accompanied by other signals and in a few minutes a number of armed men surprised the two sentinels without the mill, and having secured both their arms and their persons, made a violent attack upon the mill, broke in the window frames, and discharged a volley into the premises at the same instant.

Roused by this assault, the guard within the mill flew to arms, and discharged a heavy fire of musketry upon the assailants; this fire was returned and repeated without intermission during the conflict, the men attempting all the time to force an entrance, but without success, a number of voices crying continually 'Bank up!' 'Murder them!' 'Pull down the door!' and mixing these exclamations with the most horrid imprecations.

Again and again the attempts to make a breach were repeated, with a firmness and consistency worthy of a better cause; but every renewed attempt ended in disappointment, while the flashes from the fire–arms of the insurgents served to direct the guards to their aim. For about 90 minutes this engagement continued with undiminished fury, till at length, finding all their efforts to enter the mill fruitless, the firing and hammering without began to abate and soon after the whole body of the assailants retreated with precipitation, leaving on the field such of their wounded as could not join in the retreat.

Defence of Rawfolds Mill (*Leeds Mercury*)

An attempt was made to rally their scattered forces, to carry off their wounded, but it was in vain; the fire from within had been kept up with so much steadiness and perseverance as to produce universal dismay; during this spirited engagement 140 balls were discharged from the mill; what number of shots were fired by the mob, it is impossible to say, but the doors and windows were perforated with a vast number of pistol and musket balls, though none of them took effect, not one of the guards having sustained the least personal injury.

During the principal part of the engagement the alarm-bell was rung, and a quantity of large stones were hurled from the roof, which had an instantaneous effect, otherwise a quantity of oil of vitriol, in reserve, would have been poured down.

On the cessation of the firing, the ears of the guards were assailed with the cries of two unfortunate men, weltering in their blood, and writhing under the torture of mortal wounds:

'For God's sake,' cried one of them, 'shoot me – put me out of my misery!'

'Oh!' cried the other, 'help! Help – I know all, and I will tell all!'

One of them proved to be a cropper of the name of Samuel Hartley, formerly in the employment of Mr Cartwright; a fine-looking young unmarried man about 24 years of age, and a private in the Halifax Local Militia, in which regiment Mr

Cartwright is a captain. The other was John Booth, a youth about 19 years of age, son of a clergyman in Craven, and an apprentice to Mr Wright, of Huddersfield, a tinner. Hartley had received a shot in his left breast, apparently while making a blow at some part of the mill, which, passing through his body, had lodged beneath the skin at the left shoulder, from whence it was extracted with a portion of bone. In this situation he languished till about three o'clock on Monday morning, when he expired.

Booth's wound was in his leg, which was shattered almost to atoms; it was found necessary that he should submit to have the leg amputated; but, owing to the extreme loss of blood before the surgeons arrived, spasms came on during the operation, and he died about 6 o'clock on Sunday morning; having previously observed, that if he should recover, 'he would never be brought into such a scrape again.' It 'was observed that neither of these victims of lawless violence manifested any sense of religion.

On Monday a Coroner's Inquest assembled upon the dead bodies, and returned a Verdict of *Justifiable Homicide*. None of the wounded men, except Hartley and Booth have yet been discovered.

On the morning after the engagement, a number of hammers, axes, false keys and picklocks, with two masks, a powder-horn, and a bullet-mould were found upon the field, which was stained in several places with blood; and it is evident that many others besides those left on the field were wounded, as traces of gore were distinctly marked in every direction, and in one place to the distance of four miles. The assailants have much reason to rejoice that they did not succeed in entering the building, for we speak from our own observation when we say, that had they effected an entrance, the death of vast numbers of them from a raking fire which they could neither have returned nor controlled, would have been inevitable.

It's unnecessary to speak of the heroism of the little band that guarded these premises, there is not perhaps upon record a more distinguished instance of manly courage and cool intrepidity; but it may be proper to add, that though the assailants exceeded a hundred, the numbers opposed to them was very inconsiderable, and of that number one of the

> military conducted himself in so unsoldierlike a manner, that he was on the following morning placed in confinement, and now awaits the issue of a Regimental Court Martial.
>
> A number of reflections arise, out of this narrative, but we shall content ourselves with one remark: we have of late frequently deemed it our duty, from the regard we feel to the labouring classes, and to the laws of our country, to warn those that are engaged in those violent proceedings of the fatal consequences that await them in the unequal contest which they are now waging with the civil and military power of the country – let them reflect deeply on the late Hartley and Booth – let them recollect that they themselves may be the next victims, and let them stop in this desperate career before it is too late.

The failure at Rawfolds led to a change in Luddite tactics, starting with raids on houses, in search of money and weapons. And on April 28, William Horsfall, owner of Ottiwell's Mill in Marsden, who had announced that he would ride up to his saddle in Luddite blood, and had installed a cannon to protect his mill, was shot dead in an ambush after having stopped for his usual drink (rum and water) at the Warren House Inn and while riding along the turnpike at Crosland Moor to his home in Marsden.

The 'reluctant soldier' in Rawfolds Mill, who was said to have taken time in reloading his weapon and then 'aimed his rifle only at trees', was sentenced to be lashed on the steps of the Mill after telling his Court Martial that 'I didn't want to fire upon my brothers'. William Cartwright (who had escaped a rifle shot as he rode past Bradley Wood, in Huddersfield, the week after the assault on the mill) intervened to stop the lashing after 25 strokes had been administered.

A man named Benjamin Walker later came forward

and confessed to having taken part in Horsfall's murder, naming William Thorpe, Thomas Smith and George Mellor as co-conspirators. By turning King's evidence, Walker saved his own life. But the other three were tried and hanged in York in January 1813. The judge told the prisoners:

> 'You have been guilty of one of the greatest outrages that ever was committed in a civilised country... It is of infinite importance... that no mercy should be shown to any of you... and the sentence of the law... should be very speedily executed.'

Eight days later, 14 other men were hanged, after being rounded up for their part in the Rawfolds Mill attack. That month saw 64 men arraigned in court, of whom 24 were croppers from Huddersfield with an average age of 27. There was insufficient evidence against 30 of the accused and they were acquitted. The rest who escaped execution were sentenced to penal transportation and the harsh sentencing led to the eventual demise of the movement.

William Cartwright received donations from all parts of Yorkshire in recognition of his 'heroic actions' and by 1818 he had amassed sufficient money to buy the mill.

The Napoleonic War that lasted 12 years (culminating with the Battle of Waterloo) and a three-year war with the United States both ended in 1815. There was a brief resurgence of the Luddite movement in 1816 due to bad harvests and the depression that followed the wars, but it was soon ended by vigorous repression and rampantly reviving prosperity.

By 1820 there were no longer any traditional

croppers in employment in the West Riding. But Luddism, and that industrial revolution, had ended and steam hadn't even started in the woollen weaving industry.

This turbulent period, it is perhaps worth noting, occurred during the reign of 'mad' King George and the Regency. Both the life and reign of George III were longer than any of his predecessors and much more explosive than most. Military conflicts stretched as far afield as Africa, the Americas, India and Asia. His armies defeated France in the Seven Year's War (1756–63), effectively a battle for European (and, thereby, global) supremacy, then lost many American colonies but beat Napoleon's revolutionary France (1793–1815). And meanwhile there was history's Industrial Revolution and Luddism on the home front, the Rev Samuel Marsden's introduction of Merino wool to the King (1807), and Captain Macarthur's start of industrial export from Australia (1813).

George III was regarded as a popular monarch, far more so than his son, the Regent, who took charge from 1810 and oversaw the end of the Napoleonic war. The subsequent demobilisation of tens of thousands of men resulted in a surplus of workers on the market, which was itself in a state of over-production due to the end of hostilities.

Mile after mile of dry-stone walling was erected in Yorkshire in an effort to find jobs for veteran soldiers, but it did not solve the problem of the state of general unemployment, financial upheaval, and violently suppressed social unrest, such as the infamous uprising at Peterloo, which got its name (from Waterloo) because of the 15 deaths and 400 injuries among the civilian protesters at Peter's Fields in Manchester in 1819.

The demonstrators, frustrated by an acute economic slump, accompanied by chronic unemployment and harvest failure, and exacerbated by the Corn Laws, which kept the price of bread high, wanted the right to vote . At that time only one in ten of adult males had the vote, the fewest of them in the industrial north.

In 1820 the Regent became George IV. His reign was remarkable for his interest in matters of style and taste. It made an historic difference in both architecture and – thanks mainly to the influence of Brummell – of dress. It would, eventually, see the creation of Bradford as the centre of cloth making, yet the Regent remained an unpopular king.

Satan's Seat

Half a century behind Manchester's, came Bradford's steam-powered 'industrial revolution'. It was a revolution that meant more, not fewer jobs. The vital innovation was of the centuries-old traditions of wool–making as a traditional cottage industry being moved into vast mills.

By the middle of the 1820s Bradford was wakening from a slumber in which the actual manufacture of textiles had by-passed it. Halifax, Wakefield, Leeds, and Huddersfield had sent petitions to Parliament about the woollen trade, but Bradford might not have existed.

Its Piece Hall had been erected in 1773 but it was only a small market, and not a finishing centre. Goods were bought there 'in the white' by Leeds merchants, who took them home to be finished before export.

Even in 1818 John Aikin, in his *England Described*, devoted a mere seven lines to Bradford, compared with 30 to Halifax.

Only very slowly did the manufacture of worsteds establish itself there, but then one generation saw the transformation from a quiet little market town with industry – coal, iron and weaving – all around it, into a recognisable wool town.

With the advent of steam power and machinery,

Bradford began an explosive expansion. With the adoption and, more importantly the improvement, of machinery, and in the manufacture of new types of wool textiles, the town's clothiers started to outstrip Halifax's importance as a centre for the industry. They started to make use of the Leeds and Liverpool Canal (opened in 1774 to move coal) to import wool and to ship out their textiles.

Then the railway (1854) would put Bradford virtually on to the main line, while Halifax was left relatively isolated. Denied easy access to the main arteries of traffic, the importance of Halifax declined, and Bradford stepped up to assume recognition as the newest and most important wool town.

Its first worsted (spinning) mill had been opened in 1804 and by 1810 the town had five.

Although by the 1830s Bradford could boast of few more than twenty so-called 'worsted-producing mills' (which was something of an exaggeration because weaving itself mostly remained as an outworker cottage industry, and most of its local fabric was being sent to Leeds for finishing) its rate of development was faster than anywhere else in the country.

The success of one mill in a township encourages the opening of another, and another… Mills were the palaces of prosperity, of industry, and of employment.

For some experienced, and self-employed weavers, this would have seemed like an attractive option. No longer would they be dependent on seasons and climates (which were totally unpredictable, even before noxious chimney smoke started polluting the ozone levels). The weavers could leave their isolated cottages and meagre subsistence as farmers or farmhands or smallholders, live in a community and get steady work and regular wages all year round. True, mechanical looms needed fewer weavers, but there were more looms, and they required overseers.

There was an abundance of work for the skilled as well as for the unskilled. And plenty of opportunities for the entrepreneurs who introduced marketing and business and organisational skills to the industry. Foreign nationals built warehouses and offices so that their buyers could store and organise the shipping of the cloth they bought for export – at least half of the cloth produced in Bradford was being sold to overseas markets.

One, probably unexpected, result was the large influx of immigrant Germans.

So many of them arrived that the part of town in which they chose to live and to operate – together, because they shared a language – became known (and remains known today) as Little Germany.

The Germans were an eclectic bunch. Many of them were international merchants, frustrated by the trading impediments of the Franco-Prussian wars, who wanted to be at what was obviously now becoming the centre of the world's wool industry. They quickly built architecturally splendid neo-classical warehouses that stand today in a conservation area as a memorial to their contribution to the industry. Their part of town, bordered roughly by the Shipley–Airedale Road, Leeds

Road, Well Street and Church Bank (Barkerend Road), would become a tourist attraction – 55 of its 85 buildings are now listed as being of historical or of architectural interest.

Little Germany

Their experience of trading would expand and then dominate the selling of Bradford wool, ensuring success for the town as the new global centre.

At the same time there was an influx of Jewish weavers (and tailors), fleeing the militaristic ruling of their German state, who also made a significant contribution. A noticeable number of (non–Jewish) pork butchers arrived from Hohenlohe in south Germany, introducing factory workers – who had no time to make their own food – to the idea of fast food and takeaway eating.

People flocked into Bradford from all parts of the nation for work. Scots came because there were no jobs at home. The Irish arrived in their hundreds because the potato famine of 1845 threatened starvation. English wool workers came because it was where the jobs were.

In 1801 the population of Bradford (a town with one mill) had been 6,393, with perhaps two-thirds of them producing cheap material. But in 1851 it had grown to 52,501. If the suburbs were included the figure was 100,000 higher.

But whatever it was that they came to Bradford looking for, most of them were not going to find an easy life. The incomers, for the most part, found hard work and long hours. The pay, while promising to be regular, was low, and remained dependent upon the national economy. And the local population, unused to strangers of any kind, found life uncomfortable, working and needing to consort with so many people with strange accents or with an indecipherable language.

Sects and ghettoes were the inevitable result, as was conflict between them. Between 1830 and 1850 the most common criminal occurrence was street violence.

There were no building regulations so workers' houses were built wherever a plot of open space could be acquired. But there was no running water for them, nor any sewers, so no washing or toilet facilities. Raw sewage found its way into the Bradford Beck: a shallow stream, once fished for trout, which became a fetid fluence of filth. Overcrowding was worse, even, than in Leeds, with families often finding living space only in damp and unventilated cellars. Rubbish was thrown into the streets to join the ever increasing levels of horse manure. Rats ran everywhere. Incidences of disease –

cholera, scarlet fever, tuberculosis, smallpox, polio, rickets, and measles – were rife.

And all day the black soot from chimneys fell from the sky like heavy rain. The average life expectancy (including child deaths) within textile working families in 1850s Bradford was 18 years.

A hymn sung in Wesleyan chapels included the verse:

> On Bradford likewise look Thou down,
> Where Satan keeps his seat:
> Come, by Thy Power: Lord! him dethrone,
> For Thou art very great

And, in another:

> Sometimes there's mist and fogs that rise
> Before me in this wilderness
> Till these blow off, I cannot see
> O Lord, my God, to follow thee

In 1845 a Sanitary Commissioner reported:

> 'Taking the general condition of Bradford, I am obliged to report it to be the most filthy town I visited.'

Georg Weerth, a radical pamphleteer and friend of Marx and Engels, worked in Bradford as representative for a German textile company. In 1846 he wrote in *Neue Rheinische Zeitung* about the place:

> Every other factory town in England is a paradise in comparison to this hole. In Manchester the air lies like led upon you; in Birmingham it is just as if you were sitting with your nose in a stove pipe; in Leeds you have to cough with the dust and stink as if you have swallowed a pound of cayenne pepper in one go – but you can put up with all that. In Bradford, however, you think you have been lodged with the devil incarnate. If anyone wants to feel how the poor sinner is tormented in purgatory, let him travel to Bradford.

The more smoke and soot in the sky, the more work was in progress at ground level. The belching chimneys were the outward and visible signs of industry. The new millionaire – mostly Nonconformist – factory owners had little concern for the plight of their workers. Soot meant profit; in other words, 'Where there's muck, there's brass'. (Or, for people in the posh South: where there's muck, there's money'.)

Steam Power

Leeds has often been described as 'a city built on wool'. Bradford was, literally, a city built on coal (beneath a surface layer of clay) but it took decades for its entrepreneurs to combine the area's abundant supplies of water, iron and coal – the seam beneath Bradford extended for some 80 miles – to create steam and, from it, steam power for the county's most important industry, even though Bradford was supplying the coal and iron for Lancashire's steam powered spinning and weaving cotton mills.

In 1824 a weaver named Warwick had a powered cotton loom adapted to take worsted thread and had it installed in his mill in Shipley, supposedly as no more than an experiment. When its presence became known, handloom weavers demanded its removal and, as it was being taken away 'secretly', smashed the machinery.

In May 1826 the installation of weaving machinery at John Horsfall's North Wing Mill in Bradford and at his brother Jeremiah's Low Mill in Addingham had provoked rioting in the streets.

This was by no means a Luddite riot – it directly threatened no jobs – but it was perhaps Ludd-*ist*, in that it was against a new factory system that might threaten jobs.

The mills were however owned by dealers who generally put out their weaving to cottagers.

Rioting had broken out at the end of the previous month in Lancashire cotton mills, against the economic hardship suffered by traditional handloom weavers caused by the widespread introduction of the much more efficient power loom. It lasted for three days and ended after six rioters were shot and about 20 of the ringleaders arrested. Some of the rioters then crossed the Pennines in support of the similarly threatened Yorkshire weavers in Bradford and also in Addingham, where new power looms were being introduced.

The militia was called in when their rioting became violent and the crowd ignored instructions to disperse, until shots were fired, killing two youths. Among the special constables called in to help cope with the demonstration was 22-year-old Titus Salt, presumably already aware of the need for citizens to perform their civic duty.

The timing of the installation – of the first looms in the area to use steam- power – could hardly have been less propitious. A recession had started in 1815 at the end of the Napoleonic wars and had been exacerbated in 1825 following a stock market crash that had started with the Bank of England overspending. The wars, which had meant a boom time for employment – jobs for soldiers and sailors and in all the support industries (including, of course, an enormous demand for uniform material for the forces) – had ended, meaning that thousands of men were now without work.

Then expansionist monetary actions taken during

the transition from war to peace brought on a surge of apparent prosperity and speculative ventures. Banks caught up in the euphoria made loans that could not be supported and six London banks and 60 provincial banks – some of which printed and issued their own banknotes – were forced to close. Credit, on which the wool industry survived, was withdrawn. Banks were buying back their promissory notes at 15 shillings in the pound.

For the country weavers the earliest effect was either that there was (through no fault of their own) much less work, or far less money for the work they were doing.

When times are hard, the call for textiles for clothing is not usually a priority. Weavers might reasonably have imagined that, when the recession ended (as recessions always do, eventually) their craft skills would be replaced by machinery. It would in fact be years before steam power had any effect on the cottage-based wool weaving industry – at least not on the more conscientious and skilled and reliable home weavers – but they were not to know that.

What they did know was that a weaver who might have been paid 15 shillings for a six-day week on his own loom in 1803 was getting only five shillings (and sometimes even less) in 1818.

The situation had been exacerbated by the passing of the Corn Laws (1815) in response to a great agricultural depression in England and Wales, introduced to protect the farming landowners with a tariff on imported grain (which was cheaper and considered to be better quality than native wheat, oats and barley). The Corn Laws would occupy British politics for the next three decades (Repeal of the Corn Laws: 1846).

The Corn Laws increased the political power and influence of landowners, but they raised food prices and the cost of living for the rest of the community. The Laws hampered the growth of other economic and manufacturing sectors – most noticeably weaving – by reducing the disposable income of the public and then putting a strain on the system of poor relief that had been in effect since the first Elizabethan era.

Those weavers who could find any work at all may have counted themselves lucky in a period of general famine and chronic unemployment in which no end appeared to be in sight.

On May 1, 1826, a correspondent wrote from Skipton to the *Leeds Mercury*:

> From the best information I can collect the immediate cause of the riots is the extreme low price paid for hand weaving and the scarcity of work. The price paid to the weavers will not support his family when he is in work without parish aid. Calicoes for which 5 shillings a piece was paid for the weaving 20 years ago are now woven in some districts on the confines of Yorkshire at 10 pence a piece. and one shilling is the maximum price paid at Addingham and in this part of the country.

When times were hard the basic diet in urban areas was oatmeal with water. For those without work the options were the workhouse from which there was little likelihood of escape, or parish relief – which was a small amount of money, probably sufficient to buy little more than low– quality oatmeal for subsistence. There was no state aid: Parliament believed that local charities should support the local poor. Help did, however, come from all parts of the country from conscientious individuals who could afford charitable assistance – even, according to the *Leeds Mercury*, from the King.

The Factory System

In 1828 a group of 24 weavers in Farsley pooled their resources and bought a plot of land called The Croft. It had two or three small streams flowing through it, sufficient, at least, to power a water mill. They erected buildings for the mill, for dyeing, for scribbling and for fulling. It recruited people with the skills that they had learnt but otherwise had used only occasionally at home.

What it did not do was spinning and weaving: these vital parts of the worsted process were still being done in weavers' own homes while entrepreneurial mills were still being developed – or perhaps had already been developed – in Leeds and in Bradford.

But even home weaving was evolving. Some weavers, working long hours, often with a friend or neighbour, wove more quickly than the rest of the process could keep pace with. With a flying shuttle, two men could work two looms, instead of one or, working shifts, could keep one loom going all day. All they needed was sufficient yarn to weave.

But weavers were now working at a rate faster than they could get yarn from the spinners. And the spinners were spinning faster than the incoming supplies of raw wool. Where a weaver had a reputation for quality work, a merchant could bring in his bag of hanks of factory-spun wool to supplement the contribution of the home spinners. It was then realised that the hold-up was the final preparation of woven product before delivery to the merchant – hence the need for Farsley's Club Mill.

Along with the supply of raw (or spun) wool, the merchant would leave a cash deposit, and get a firm date for collection and full payment for woven (but still 'unfinished') pieces: the 'piece rate'.

In many cases the master weaver started sourcing his own spun yarn, or buying raw wool from farmers, using operators like the Club Mill to prepare it, and employing women to spin it. Then they would send the woven cloth back to the Club Mill for fulling. There had been fulling mills along the same river in 1373.

The Farsley fulling facility was basically a service industry, open to all, but used mostly by its owners. Its success was guaranteed because the weavers produced cloth at a faster rate than traditional household scribbling of the raw wool and fulling, tentering and dyeing of the fabric could keep up with.

The Club Mill project, communally owned, developed at an enormous rate, doubling its size after five years (in 1833).

Once Yorkshire had started to fully recognise the value of steam to power its looms (around 1850), it seemed logical to bring weaving in-house. In 1882 the entire business was sold to Edwin Woodhouse, a Halifax mill-owner, and the Club Mill would become better known, later, as Sunny Bank Mills, with family names including Hainsworth, Ross and Gaunt appearing on its headed notepaper.

Even slower than the West Riding to take up steam power – and lacking the important benefits of fast–running soft water, and local coal and iron supplies – the wool industry diminished in Devon, Somerset, Wiltshire Norfolk and Gloucestershire. Yorkshire's 'Wool District' – with a reputation for paying lower wages – became the place for cloth.

In the middle of the 19th century new custom-built powered mills were being erected throughout West Yorkshire but they did not work any faster than the typical and experienced handloom weaver (the rate being weaving through 40 warps a minute). The big difference was that powered looms produced wool not by the yard, but by the mile.

There was, clearly, employment and (at least) a living wage for many, and even wealth for a few. But there was nothing remarkable about the quality of the production of either wool or textiles in the Ridings, apart, perhaps, from their remarkable lack of any great 'quality'. But there was plenty of it, and it was cheap.

It was only when they started to use fine, long-haired fleeces from Lincolnshire sheep – shortly before the introduction of Merino – that the West Riding wool product would improve.

Vertically Challenged

It was Benjamin Gott who had the inspirational idea of bringing all the manufacturing processes together under one roof in his two mills in Leeds. There were more than 30 separate procedures involved in converting parts of a fleece into a saleable piece of cloth.

These included: the sorting, separating, grading and selection of the fibres, washing (separating the lanolin) and drying, dyeing, carding and combing, twisting and spinning and reeling, and aligning the warps on a beam. Then there was the choice (and colour) of the weft thread, and then interlacing (weaving) the horizontal through the vertical threads. And after that the scouring with fullers' earth, burling to pick out irregular threads and hairs, fulling with soap and warm water, tentering, teaseling, and shearing the nap, pressing, burling to remove defects, again, inspecting and pressing and packing, ready for the warehouse and the cloth hall.

He had created the 'vertical mill' meaning that the raw wool went into it, and finished cloth came out. In the early endeavours, the raw wool (being lightweight) was handled on the upper floors and the shuddering and heavy weaving machinery on the ground floors and trapdoors in the floors in between – hence, 'vertical'.

Manufacturers travelled from all parts of Europe to

see Gott's mills in action, but despite the profitability of the enterprise, others were slow to follow his lead until the period of exponential industrial and economic growth of the 1820s, when huge numbers of woollen mills were built in the town.

Gott's success meant less work being produced on cottage looms, and in the 1820s the number of individual sellers at the Cloth Market would reduce by half.

Nevertheless it would take time before the machine loom could beat the quality of the best home-weavers, who blithely continued to have their own wool cleaned, dyed, carded and spun, before weaving on their own looms, and then sending it to the local mill where it would be fulled, washed and tentered. It was then taken in what was called its balk state to the Cloth Hall to be sold by merchants who would have it finished and dressed to their liking.

When Gott got going, around the start of the 1800s, the population of Leeds was 58,000. By 1851 it had more or less trebled to 172,000 (with 38,000 houses). But the 'Leeds Clothing District' – which meant the villages around it – included a further 105,000 people which considerably increased the town's importance.

According to mid-century factory reports there were 340 firms operating 2,344 power looms, 23,328 workers in factories and 17,000 contributing to the industry from their homes – a total of more than 42,000 people. Somebody even counted the spindles: there were 423,482 in 'the Leeds district'.

Despite all this industry, Leeds would essentially

remain a marketing, rather than a manufacturing town, Though small in size (there was no official census until 1801), Leeds had long been established as the 'ancient seat of woollen manufacture'. In 1715 Ralph Thoresby, an historian of repute, wrote that *Leedes* (which he insisted was the original and correct spelling) 'was deservedly celebrated both at home and in the most distant trading parts of Europe for the woollen manufacture'. And he described the 'famous cloth market' as 'the life, not of the town alone, but of these parts of England'.

The next Clothing District in importance in the mid-1800s was Huddersfield.

Bradford was still a coal town with wool mills in it. But it was expanding its importance by leaps and bounds.

Dark Satanic Mills

While most of Yorkshire hesitated over the introduction of new technologies that were already revolutionising the cotton industry a few miles away, Benjamin Gott was getting on with it.

His father, the engineer for the Aire and Calder Navigation (by which the Aire was made navigable from Goole docks to Leeds and the Calder to Wakefield) and later surveyor for the West Riding, bought him, first, an apprenticeship at eighteen, and then a partnership with Wormald and Fountaine, a leading firm of Leeds cloth merchants. When the senior partners died Gott took over full control.

In 1792 at the age of 30, he bought a piece of parkland known as Bean Ing ('Ing' meaning meadow), next to the river at the end of the street in which the Coloured Cloth Hall was situated, but which at the time was still in open country. The Park had been considered a smart address for the middle classes since the first houses had been built in the 1760s; it was close enough to the centre of town to walk there and back for business. Gott began building a new mill (originally called Park Mill) where many of the processes of cloth making could be brought together and mechanised – including weaving by steam power.

He bought new machinery and installed one of the newly developed Boulton and Watt steam engines, forging a lasting friendship with the inventors (engineer Matthew Boulton and inventor James Watt) and buying their patents. He also experimented with cloth finishing methods and dyeing processes (a dyehouse had been the only industry in the immediate vicinity of Bean Ing).

By 1800 the mill had 38 scribbling and carding machines (the average mill would have only about half a dozen) and was employing more than a thousand workers while the wars with France, which had started in 1793, forced a recession affecting most routine textile trading, but bringing a sudden heavy call for army uniform cloth and blankets from Gott's mill. Trade with the Americas and China was also booming.

It became impossible to meet demand, and in 1804 he bought another vast mill at Armley. The site of a fulling mill since 1590, it had been severely damaged by fire when Gott bought the ruins, so he ordered that the rebuilding include cast iron internal frames and joists and other fire-retarding measures. When the repairs were completed in 1805, the new mill was the largest wool factory in the world, and Leeds was now definitively the world's textile industry centre.

Visitors from all over Europe marvelled at Gott's increasingly massive Armley and Bean Ing mills.

Within a decade or so Gott had changed the nature of Leeds from a vital commercial hub into an important industrial centre.

In the process he made a fortune, buying and building a great mansion and park (now the Leeds City municipal golf course). He also sponsored buildings and works of art and built alms-houses for the town. Although he had shifted from merchant to manufacturer, guaranteeing the supply of cloth that he then traded, he described himself as a merchant because in Leeds the cloth merchants had a higher, much more gentlemanly, social status. When he died in 1840 he was a millionaire.

Benjamin Gott

Steam power required coal and coal produced

smoke and soot, which blew and settled all over the town (Leeds achieved 'city' status in 1893).

Smoke was first recognised as a public nuisance in London in 1819 and parliament passed the UK's first clean air ('smoke nuisance') legislation in 1821.

For many, the sight of plumes of smoke from industrial chimneys was a sign of prosperity. But for others, finding soot in their hair, on their clothing, on their vegetables and even seeping through their window frames, it was a menace with which, it seemed, they were doomed to live.

In 1818 a reader of the *Leeds Mercury* complained about ashes – 'the pulverised refuse of the steam engine and dye–house' – being used for pavements in place of sand, while 'smoke and soot in abundance are evils inseparable from our situation'.

The letter seemed to imply (or to state directly) that, while ashes for the pavements were causing 'no little inconvenience', the presence of smoke and soot had become a fact of life in Leeds.

It may have been the first mention of smoke and soot in the public press in Leeds, but it hardly rated as a complaint. However the 'nuisance' had been sufficiently apparent for parliament to have noticed and the invention and appliance of patent 'smoke burners' — by which smoke was passed back and burnt off by the fire before cleaner emissions would emerge from mill chimneys – began to appear.

In 1820 the *Mercury* congratulated the efforts of various inventors discovering ways –

> 'to remove the increasing and almost intolerable nuisance, arising from the smoke of Steam Engines and Furnaces, with

which the air of this and all the other manufacturing towns of the kingdom is at present contaminated, and are likely to be crowned with success'.

The newspaper hoped that –

'there is public spirit enough in the proprietors of the manufacturies, dye-houses and furnaces in the populous towns and villages of Yorkshire as well as other counties forthwith to direct their attention to the removal of the prevailing evil which by its blighting influence upon vegetation shows but too clearly what must be its effects upon the constitution of every man woman and child whose misfortune it is to be obliged to breathe this impure atmosphere'.

It added that

'It is probable however that some expense may attend the alteration of the steam engine and other furnaces already erected, but that is an obstacle which no man who has a proper regard to the public health and comfort will suffer to stand in the way of the removal of this pestilential nuisance.'

Although one persuasive claim was that one smoke-consuming invention reduced the consumption of fuel by a quarter, and another invention reduced it to a quarter, mill owners were generally unimpressed and slow to react. A mill in Bramley experimented with a smoke burner without noticing any benefit.

In 1822 the *Mercury* reported:

'It has often been urged in extenuation of the nuisance created by the suffocating smoke from steam-engine chimneys, that no plan has yet been discovered, by which this evil could be removed; and this plea, if well founded, would be entitled to due consideration; but it is not well founded. Several plans have been devised, many of them calculated to diminish the dense clouds in which manufacturing places are now so frequently involved....'

The report cited one mill with a successful smoke burning appliance:

'...This has been done at a small expense and, we believe, with the saving of fuel, but the saving is not the question. No man has the right to contaminate the air which the public breathes, though he should not save anything by keeping it pure.'

One month later the same newspaper described the success of Bradford smoke abatement and wrote that:

'We have to congratulate the inhabitants of Bradford upon the success of their efforts to free the town from the nuisance created by the smoke of steam engine chimneys. Though the numerous manufactories in that place are in a state of great activity, there is not thrown up by all the steam engine furnaces in that town in the course of a day as much smoke as is emitted from one of the engines in Leeds in a single hour. By what means this salutary change has been effected we are not accurately informed, but it is a subject worthy of enquiry and affords an example that cannot be too soon followed in other places.'

Which was all very well, except that in the first 20 years of the century Bradford had gone from having only one textile mill to (comparatively only) 20 mills.

Whereas in 1822 the *Leeds Intelligencer* reported that

'we have, in the township of Leeds, ninety steam-engines; about fifty of which are entirely without burners, about thirty with inefficient burners, and not more than ten or twelve with efficient burners.'

If the *Mercury* had investigated thoroughly it would have easily discovered the 'salutary' difference. Since 1803 the Bradford Improvement Act had required that

'Engine chimneys are to be erected of sufficient height as not to create a nuisance by the emission of smoke. All owners of engines etc. are to construct fireplaces thereof in such a manner as most effectually to destroy and consume the smoke arising therefrom.'

Bradford had other coal-fired smoke – and soot – producing factories on the outskirts of the town (it became a city in 1897, four years after Leeds) in the form of mines and foundries, and major ironworks at Bowling, Low Moor and Shelf. At the turn of the century it had not needed smoke and steam for its non-existent textile industry.

The middle classes in Leeds were relatively mobile: the residents of the Park Estate moved, first, to higher ground at Woodhouse Lane, and then upwind to the suburbs of Headingley, Alwoodley, Woodhouse Moor and Meanwood. They could use carriages or ride horses to get into town when necessary.

The working classes – the people manning the mills – needed to live within walking distance, and the more affordable properties were downwind, in the smoke. These people mostly lived in squalor, often in overcrowded single-room accommodation where they both cooked and slept. There was no running water and no sanitation: their waste buckets were emptied out into the street. The indoor and outdoor stench of urban living was consequently vile.

When natural air movement was relatively still, thick heavy smoke drew a blanket of fog over the stinking streets.

Committees were formed, meetings were held and speeches were made. Something had to be done. An advertisement in the *Leeds Mercury* warned that factory owners who did not install smoke consumers would face prosecution by a newly formed Committee For The Consumption Of Smoke.

In 1823, for a population of about 84,000. there were nearly 130 industrial coal-fired steam engines in mills in and around the town (by 1830 there would be 225), plus 25 coal-consuming dyehouses.

Five Leeds mill owners – those who were alleged to

be producing the most smoke – were accused of criminal neglect, in that they had not adopted smoke consuming systems.

Four of them decided to install burners to avoid trial. Only one, Benjamin Gott, decided to fight the case on the grounds that the contraptions, and the arguments for them, were 'an utter folly'. He asked for the trial to be moved from Leeds Quarter Sessions to Westminster, claiming that a Leeds jury would be prejudiced, and eventually it was moved instead to the Court of King's Bench at York.

The new location, some 25 miles distant from Leeds, was an inconvenience for the prosecution who had to produce witnesses in court, using either the Highflyer, or the Royal Sovereign, stagecoaches that had to change their horses at Wetherby.

When the trial was relocated the committee suddenly decided that the smoke produced by Gott's mill had recently been considerably reduced and asked to stop the litigation. They asked the court, instead, for costs (against Gott) for the preparation of their case. That was a mistake.

Gott's response was a flat refusal to pay – on the grounds that claims of any recent reduction of smoke emitted from his chimneys were untrue because he had not changed anything. Relocating to York had been no problem for Gott, who was prepared to devote both time and money fighting his case and who had no wish to make life easy for his accusers. The trial went ahead.

The committee then had second (or third) thoughts and the case against Gott, when the trial opened in 1824, was now straightforward. His steam engines were emitting noxious fumes of smoke and soot that polluted the town, to the detriment of the inhabitants because he had neglected to install smoke consuming equipment in his mills.

That was another mistake by his accusers.

Much was made of the fact that Gott himself lived a couple of miles distant in Armley, enjoying pure air, while in sight of his own chimneys that produced the 'smoke nuisance' for citizens elsewhere.

But Gott pointed out that when the sky was filled with clouds of black smoke it was impossible to judge from which chimneys the worst of it came. He insisted that the main cause of the 'nuisance' was the factories that were newer than his. He pointed out that his factory had been built in the middle of a field in 1792 and people had chosen to build houses in the meadow around it.

He had, furthermore, built his factory next to a dye-house that had been operating before the Park Estate was planned in the 1760s. The dyehouse was the largest in Leeds and produced vast amounts of smoke from the 20 wagons – 50 tons – of coal that it consumed every week. There was a white long-horned cow on the premises in the tenting croft and the dairyman had to wash it regularly as it started appearing grey, or even black. Evidence was given that the dyehouse produced five times more smoke than Gott's chimneys. The owner of the dyehouse had asked Gott's engineer, 'How is it you make less smoke than I do, although I have got one of these new smoke burners?'

And yet, in spite of the so-called 'nuisance'. the estate had become a prestigious address within Leeds.

At the time of the trial there was absolutely no medical evidence that the ingesting of industrial smoke might be injurious to health – even if the smoke abatement committee thought that it must be obvious. People complained that sometimes they could not see across the streets as great clouds of smoke rolled along them. They had soot on their clothes, their vegetables and their windowsills and often within their houses. But that was as far as the 'nuisance' could factually go.

Presumably when he eventually tired of what he must have considered to have been a ludicrous and time-wasting legal charade, Gott produced the first ace from his sleeve.

His defence counsel called on medical opinions from two respected surgeons at the Leeds General Infirmary. A Mr Chorley said he was 'quite sure that the smoke from the defendant's mill is not prejudicial to the health of the neighbourhood'. He did not consider 'smoke in its simple state, unmixed with the vapours of deleterious ingredients and in the quantities usually made in manufacturing towns to be generally unfavourable to health'.

He was of the opinion that –

> 'the central part of Leeds is much more unhealthy than the neighbourhood of the defendant's mill — the smoke there being very much greater in quantity, and mixed with the noxious effluvia arising from a crowded population.'

Mr Chorley claimed that it was –

> 'a typical view of the medical profession that coal smoke is not unwholesome, and vapour from a crowded living environment is more problematic.'

What Mr Chorley was saying, in effect, was that the overcrowded workers' houses, with a prevailing stench of squalor within them. might benefit from a healthy waft of honest smoke passing through them.

Mr Chorley's opinion was supported by a second surgeon at the Infirmary, a Mr Hey, who 'thought that the accusation that air in the neighbourhood of the defendant's mill is corrupted and unwholesome is quite preposterous'.

Gott had another ace. The inventor of the smoke burner he (allegedly) had criminally neglected to install was generally recognised to have been one William Prichard. So eager had Gott been to do what was best for society he had employed the man as his own mill engineer to install and operate the new equipment. But the installation had not produced any improvement and textile production at the mill had to be stopped frequently while further expensive adjustments were made to it. Finally, Gott had dismissed Prichard on the simple basis that his invention did not work.

Since 1799, in fact, Gott had been heating his scouring and dyeing vessels under the direction of his good friends Matthew Boulton and James Watt, which had reduced the number of fires required from 40 to only two. And these two fireplaces had been constructed on the basis of Watt's patent for reducing smoke, by which they were (as far as was possible) 'made mutually to consume each other's smoke'.

The only time since 1799 when Watt's invention had not been wholly in use was when Prichard's ineffective invention had been tried.

A jury found Gott not guilty of having criminally neglected to install smoke burners to reduce the nuisance of smoke detrimental to the public.

And the smoke rolled on (albeit, perhaps, not so very much of it from Mr Benjamin Gott's mills.)

The committee would not know it – although they might well have guessed it – but Leeds was in process of becoming the filthiest, smokiest, most polluted town in Europe. And steam-powered weaving had not even fully started yet.

The dense smoke was to be a symbol of world-beating industrialisation, but a dubious distinction that would prevail for more than a century.

Reform

John Wood was born in Bradford in 1793, the son of a successful manufacturer of tortoiseshell combs in Ivegate. At 15 he was apprenticed to Richard Smith, the town's biggest spinner of worsted yarn, but in 1815 when his father extended his own premises, in which he used steam power, he took over part of the factory and went into business on his own account, as a (steam-powered) spinner.

A powered loom was introduced in 1826 – one of the first in Bradford.

In the linear clothing district, roughly from Leeds to the far side of Bradford, there were an estimated 6,000 maisters (recognised experienced master weavers) who provided employment for between 30,000 and 40,000 other clothiers at the start of the 1800s.

The numbers decreased with the introduction of the factory system, and with the employment of women and children, paid less than the men, who were often depicted as hanging about, useless jobless, and shamed by having to depend on their wives and children for a family income.

Because the new textile technology was 'so simple that even a child could do it', that is what the mill-owners were doing... employing children at a fraction of the wages they would have had to pay the parents, while putting the adults out of work.

The preliminary stages of the process – the sorting, breaking, cleaning and fulling, and in some cases the dyeing of the raw wool – everything that happened before the actual spinning, was still very much a cottage industry. Most of the mills were spinning mills, but once weaving became mechanised there was no holding Bradford back.

Leeds had always been the centre for woollens, but it also had flax, canvas, linen, sacking and thread production. Bradford was going to weave the world's worsteds; Leeds could look after the rest.

It was boom time for Bradford. Mill after mill was erected in local sandstone, each one bigger and more impressive than the last, their stylish chimneys towering up to 250 feet, mindful of the town's clean air act.

There was plenty of work for those who wanted it, and families (especially those with children, for whom work was virtually guaranteed) had begun to pour into the West Riding from all parts of the nation.

So far, it would seem, so good. But the palatial outer architecture of the mills belied the insides, and working life was grim. The hours were long and the work was arduous and unrelenting. The unguarded machinery was dangerous for the children who ducked and dived around it, while it was still in motion, to keep the floors clean (because wool dust was a constant fire risk).

What mattered to the manufacturers was profit, first

and foremost. Conditions under which the workers toiled was of little or no concern to most mill owners, many of whom were becoming millionaires.

John Wood's business also expanded faster even than the rest of Bradford and by 1828 he was employing 500 workers – many of them children – and was thus recognised as one of the most successful worsted spinners in Britain, and therefore, probably, in the world..

He may have been something of a pioneer, but he was not keen on the way his chosen industry was progressing.

He wrote:

> Little children in my mills work from six in the morning to seven o'clock in the evening. In some mills in the neighbourhood little children are working 14, 15, 16 and even 18 hours a day without a single minute having been set apart for meals. Besides all this, in many mills they are cheated out of portions of their scanty wages by fines and other means of fraud.

Wood believed that this was socially and morally reprehensible, but nevertheless did the same, himself. Having tried and failed to persuade his fellow mill owners to agree to employ adults rather than children, or even at least to reduce the length of the working day and improve conditions for them, he was aware that to go it alone would put him at a disadvantage in competitive pricing.

Officially, the prevailing hours for working in the Bradford worsted industry were 6am to 7pm, with a 30–minute break for lunch: Wood was credited with being the first employer to allow time for breakfast.

The mills also imposed a system of financial

penalties for minor mistakes or misbehaviour, thereby reducing the children's already meagre pay packets, and of overseers inflicting harsh corporal punishment.

> **Rules to be observed by the hands in this mill**
>
> 1. Any person coming too late shall be fined as follows: for five minutes 2d, ten minutes 4d, 15 minutes 6d.
>
> 2. A fine of 1d for every bobbin found on the floor.
>
> 3. For any waste on the floor, 2d.
>
> 4. A fine of 2d for anyone not oiling the machines at the correct time.
>
> 5. Any person leaving their work and found talking with other workers shall be fined 2d for each offence.
>
> 6. A fine of 3d for insolent language. If it happens again the worker shall be dismissed.
>
> 7. The machinery shall be swept and cleaned down every meal time.
>
> 8. All workers shall give four weeks notice if they want to leave their employment. But [the employer] does not need to give any notice before dismissing a worker.
>
> 9. The Masters would recommend that all their workpeople should wash themselves every morning and any found not washing will be fined 3d.
>
> 10. Any person damaging this notice will be dismissed.

On October 16, 1830, Wood asked his friend Richard Oastler, a man locally well known for his support of (Hull–born) William Wilberforce in abolishing slavery, to visit his mill and help solve the problem.

He told him:

> You are very enthusiastic against slavery in the West Indies and I assure you there are cruelties daily practised in our mills on little children which if you knew about I am sure you would strive to prevent.

Oastler's reaction to this visit was most seriously felt in Bradford, but only because that was where Wood's mill was located and from where he reported what he saw. But he was under no illusion about the terrible conditions he observed being restricted to the one mill or even to a single town. Immediately on returning home he penned the first of a series of damning letters to the *Leeds Mercury* headed YORKSHIRE SLAVERY (that is, not 'Bradford slavery') in which he described what he had witnessed that day:

> Let truth speak out, appalling as the statement may appear. Thousands of our fellow creatures and fellow subjects, both male and female, the miserable inhabitants of a Yorkshire town, are this very moment existing in a stage of slavery more horrid than are victims of that hellish system 'Colonial Slavery'. These innocent creatures drawl out unpitied their short but miserable existence in a place famed for its profession of religious zeal, whose inhabitants are ever foremost in professing Temperance and Reformation, and are striving to outrun their neighbours in Missionary exertions and would fain send the Bible to the farthest corner of the globe... The very streets which receive the droppings of an Anti– Slavery Society are every morning wet by the tears of innocent victims at the accursed shrine of avarice, who are compelled not by the cart whip or the negro slave–driver but by the dread of the equally appalling thong or the strap of the overlooker, to hasten, half–dressed, not half–fed, to those magazines of

> British infantile slavery – the worsted mills in the town and neighbourhood of Bradford. Thousands of little children, both male and female, but principally female, from SEVEN to fourteen years of age, are daily compelled to labour from six o'clock in the morning to seven in the evening...Poor infants! Ye are indeed sacrificed at the shrine of avarice, without even the solace of the negro slave; ...ye are compelled to work as long as the necessity of your needy parents may require, or the cold-blooded avarice of your worse than barbarian masters may demand!

This and subsequent letters were met with denial and criticism; but he established their truth:

> I had lived for many years in the very heart of the factory districts. I had been on terms of intimacy and of friendship with many factory masters, and I had all the while fancied that factories were blessings to the poor.

He collected more and similar evidence from other mills and began his campaign for a maximum ten- hour working day.

In 1831 Oastler wrote a long letter to the *Mercury* reiterating the need for factory regulation. In it, he criticised the hypocrisy of the people who opposed colonial slavery while treating their own native children in a worse way. The *Mercury* printed his letter but edited it, telling readers it had not printed the full letter because it 'outraged the judgement' and 'exceeded the bounds of reason and justice', and contained 'brimstone rhetoric'. Oastler sent a copy to the *Leeds Intelligencer*, the great (Tory) rival of the (Whig) *Mercury*, which was happy to print the letter in full.

Thereafter he favoured the *Intelligencer*, which would later become the (Conservative) *Yorkshire Post*.

He created so much attention that he was called to give evidence to a Parliamentary Select Committee.

He told it:

> On one occasion I was very singularly placed; I was in the company of a West India slave master and three Bradford spinners; they brought the two systems into fair comparison, and the spinners were obliged to be silent when the slave-owner said, "well, I have always thought myself disgraced by being the owner of black slaves, but we never, in the West Indies, thought it was possible for any human being to be so cruel as to require a child of 9 years old to work 12½ hours a day; and that, you acknowledge, is your regular practice."
>
> I have seen little boys and girls of 10 years old, one I have in my eye particularly now, whose forehead has been cut open by the thong; whose cheeks and lips have been laid open, and whose back has been almost covered with black stripes; and the only crime that that little boy, who was 10 years and 3 months old, had committed, was that he retched three cardings, which are three pieces of woollen yarn, about three inches long.
>
> The same boy told me that he had been frequently knocked down with the billy-roller, and that on one occasion, he had been hung up by a rope round the body, and almost frightened to death...
>
> I have seen their bodies almost broken down, so that they could not walk without assistance, when they have been 17 or 18 years of age...

Oastler went on to contrast the factory system with the form of domestic manufacturing in the West Riding that he remembered from his youth:

> It was the custom for the children at that time to mix learning their trades with other instruction and with amusement, and they learned their trades or their occupations, not by being put into places, to stop there from morning to night, but by having a little work to do, and then some time for instruction, and they were generally under the immediate care of their parents.
>
> The villages about Leeds and Huddersfield were occupied by respectable little clothiers, who could manufacture a piece of cloth or two in the week, or three or four or five pieces, and always had their family at home. They could at that time make a good profit by what they sold; there were filial

> affection and parental feeling, and not over-labour.
>
> But that race of manufacturers has been almost completely destroyed. There are scarcely any of the old-fashioned domestic manufacturers left, and the villages are composed of one or two or in some cases of three or four, mill owners, and the rest, poor creatures, who are reduced and ground down to want, and in general are compelled to live upon the labour of their little ones. It is almost the general system for the little children in these manufacturing villages to know nothing of their parents at all excepting that in a morning very early, at 5 o'clock, very often before 4, they are awakened by a human being that they are told is their father, and are pulled out of bed – I have heard many a score of them give an account of it – when they are almost asleep, and lesser children are absolutely carried on the backs of the older children asleep to the mill. They see no more of their parents till they go home at night, and are sent to bed.
>
> The general effect of the system is this, and they know it, to place a bonus upon crimes; because their little children, and their parents too, know that if they only commit theft and break the laws, they will be taken up and put into the House of Correction, and there they will not have to work more than 6 or 7 hours a day.

His campaign had some effect. The 1833 Factories Act prohibited the employment in textile factories of children under nine years of age. It limited the hours of 9-to 13-year-olds to nine hours a day and of children between 13 and 18 to no more than 12 hours. Children were not to work at night and two hours of schooling a day was to be provided for them.

But this was not enough for Oastler who pointed out that only four factory inspectors were being appointed to enforce the law, therefore many mill owners were likely to ignore it. And he was right about that. A factory inspector's report to Parliament in 1836 showed that:

> I took the evidence from the mouths of the boys themselves. They stated to me that they commenced working on Friday morning, the 27th of May last, at 6am, and that, with the exception of meal hours and one hour at midnight extra, they did not cease working till four o'clock on Saturday evening, having been two days and a night thus engaged.
>
> Believing the case scarcely possible, I asked every boy the same questions, and from each received the same answers. I then went into the house to look at the time book, and in the presence of one of the masters, referred to the cruelty of the case, and stated that I should certainly punish it with all the severity in my power.

In 1844 the Act reduced the hours of work for children between 8 and 13 to six and a half hours a day, either in the morning or afternoon, no child being allowed to work in both on the same day, except on alternate days, and then to work only for ten hours. Children and women (now included for the first time) were to have the same hours, that is, not more than twelve for the first five days of the week (with one and a half hours allowed for meals), and nine hours on Saturday, and no night-working.

All dangerous machinery was to be securely fenced off, and failure to do so would be regarded as a criminal offence. No child or young person was to clean mill machinery while it was in motion. It was, in effect, Britain's first health and safety legislation.

But Oastler was still campaigning for a ten-hour limit for women and children. He made speeches, with plenty of public enthusiasm but without any great effect, urging voters not to elect parliamentary candidates who opposed his campaign, but meanwhile failing (by 22 votes) to be elected himself.

He was supported in the Commons by Lord Ashley

(later Earl of Shaftesbury) and after many rejections a ten-hour law – sometimes known as Lord Ashley's Act – was passed… in 1847, 17 years after Oastler's campaign had started.

The Act prohibited the employment of children under the age of eight and restricted the working hours in textile mills of women and children (under 18) to ten hours a day.

Oastler died, bankrupt, in 1861 and was buried in the family vault at Kirkstall. Twelve factory workers carried his coffin and hundreds of mill workers, factory hands and families with children attended as did a number of mill owners, MPs, lawyers and churchmen. The entombment was held at lunchtime, and the congregation stayed at the church until being called back to work by the factory bells.

In his native Leeds he has a plaque.

More than £1,500 was raised by public subscription in 1869 to build a bronze statue in his honour which was erected in Northgate, Bradford.

A memorial to Lord Shaftesbury would be erected in Piccadilly Circus, London, in 1893. Topped by a statue entitled 'the Angel of Christian Charity', it has become popularly, albeit mistakenly, known as *Eros*.

This engraving of Richard Oastler was distributed with copies of the *Northern Star*, December 12, 1840

In 1925 prime minister Stanley Baldwin, while visiting Leeds, described Richard Oastler as 'the first of those who had conferred distinction on the city', saying:

> 'It was in this city that he was born and Leeds will always be linked with his name. And yet it is to be feared that many of its citizens do not know his name.'

Perhaps as a direct result of that reference, in the same year West Leeds High School (which had opened in 1907) introduced the 'house' system for pupils. Its four houses were named after some of the more famous names associated with the city: De Lacy (land-owner – history), Priestley (the 'discoverer' of oxygen – science), Hook (Bishop of Leeds and educational activist – learning) and Oastler himself (representing industry), It is doubtful whether even boys in Oastler house knew the extent of his achievements.

Master and Man

While it still remains arguable about whatever it was and whenever the 'industrial revolution' occurred, there can be no doubt at all that the Victorian era (1837-1901) was the Industrial Age...the age of transport moving everything from coal and iron and stone to fine worsteds by means of canals and railways and horse-cart along busy waterways, new railroads and half-decent roads... an age of building, warehouses and mills with opulent frontages and workers' housing with front aspects but with no back doors ...an age of innovation and development...an age of social enlightenment... and, eventually, an age of political change.

Victoria's Britain could justifiably claim to be the first world superpower, despite severe social inequality at home.

Most notably of all, it was the age that defined the stark difference between Master – the mill owners who would make and sometimes lose, and then make again, millions of pounds – and Man, as the downtrodden worker. As Benjamin Disraeli put it (albeit it in a novel):

> Two nations between whom there is no intercourse and no sympathy; who are ignorant of each other's habits, thoughts and feelings, as if they were dwellers in different zones or inhabitants of different planets; who are formed by different breeding, are fed by different food, are ordered by different manners, and are not governed by the same laws ... THE RICH AND THE POOR.

In Leeds, in 1801, about 40 per cent of the 53,302 population lived outside the actual township. A cholera outbreak in 1832 caused the authorities to address the problems of drainage, sanitation, and water supply.

In 1841, by which time the population had expanded to 150,234, only 2,000 houses had running water and consequently the *Intelligencer* reported that the River Aire was

> '...charged with the contents of about 200 water closets and similar places, a great number of common drains, the drainings from dunghills, the Infirmary (dead leeches, poultices for patients, etc), slaughter houses, chemical soap, gas, dung, dyehouses and manufactures, spent blue and black dye, pig manure, old urine wash, with all sorts of decomposed animal and vegetable substances from an extent of drainage between Armley Mills to the Kings Mill amounting to about 30,000,000 gallons per annum of the mass of filth with which the river is loaded.'

The following year a *Report on the Sanitary Conditions of the Labouring Population of Great Britain* included evidence from Robert Baker, a Leeds doctor and town councillor, that

> 'Of the 586 streets in Leeds, 68 only are paved by the town... Of those 68, 19 are not sewered at all, and 10 only partly so... It is only within the last three of four years past that a sewer has been completed through the main street for two of the most populous wards (a population of 30,540 persons) ...
>
> Here and there stagnant water, and channels so offensive that they have been declared to be unbearable, lie under the doorways of the uncomplaining poor...'

Baker also reported that:

> 'In one cul-de-sac... there are 34 houses, and in ordinary times, there dwell in these houses 340 persons, or ten to every house; but as these houses are many of them receiving houses for itinerant labourers, during the periods of hay-time and harvest and the fairs, at least twice that number are then here

congregated. The name of this place is the Boot and Shoe Yard, in Kirkgate, a location from whence the Commissioners removed, in the days of cholera, 75 cart-loads of manure, which had been untouched for years, and where there now exists a surface of human excrement of very considerable extent, to which these impure and unventilated dwellings are additionally exposed.'

Baker's research had been unremitting. He had found one

'...dark and dank cellar, inhabited by Irish families, including pigs, with broken panes in every window–frame, and filth and vermin in every nook. Here with walls un–whitewashed for years, black with the smoke of foul chimneys, without water... sacking for bed–clothing, with floors unwashed from year to year, without out–offices, and with incomes of a few shillings a week, derived from the labour of half-starved children or the more precarious earnings of casual employment...'

It was an age of chimneys, piercing the skyline that – because of the amount of smoke being emitted – was often impossible to see.

All classes – that is, anybody who needed to go into Leeds – suffered from the smoke and soot. They were ingesting air that they could see; their skin and their clothes were permeated with the smell of smoke, every doorknob or handle, every surface, that they touched, blackened their hands; blowing their noses blackened their handkerchiefs, their hair was matted with spider–webs of soot.

It was period of high employment – jobs a-plenty, but also so many jobseekers flocking into the West Riding for them that wages were kept low.

An estimated 14,000 handloom weavers were still working in West Yorkshire in 1838, roughly ten years after the advent of power weaving, about 4,000 in Leeds itself and another 4,500 in the surrounding area, while about 200 power looms were operating in the borough.

Twenty years later there were still cottagers who were working their looms at home, in contradiction of fears that they would either go out of business or be driven into the mills to operate the new power looms.

While it is obviously difficult to state what might be the 'average' income for a good home weaver, or even to try to define one, various reports suggest that it might have been around ten shillings a week in 1838, roughly the same as it had been in 1780. At the same time, the pay for a factory worker was not much different: 11s for a weaver but up to 13s for a 'good weaver' or overseer.

Similarly, there are no records of earnings of home spinners, while in Bradford spinning mills an overseer of up to 40 children might be paid about 22s in 1823. Eight-year-old children would be on 2s a week, their wages increasing by 6d a year.

By 1857 women weavers outnumbered the men and wages had risen to about 13s for a 56½-hour week.

In 1800 a shepherd, average, got £16 a year; in 1850, £25.

The paybook for Waterloo Mills in Pudsey (where no weaving was done) shows that on an average week in 1851, dyers and scourers of wool earned 21 to 25 shillings; fullers were paid 22s and tenterers 21; spinners earned 25s. Children under 13 (28 of them) received 2s a week, increasing by 6d each year.

The Mills employed 120 weavers, but 'not on the premises', who were paid 14s a week.

The fabric would then go, in its unfinished state, for sale at Leeds Cloth Hall.

Prevailing winds would blow Bradford's noxious soot and smoke towards Leeds, although in fact, in spite of the chimneys' height, most of the soot fell into the town, somewhere – maybe a few hundred yards away from the originating mill.

The new industry and the prosperity it produced meant that there were jobs in abundance for workers outside the clothing industry.

The factories needed bankers, accountants, lawyers and architects, engineers and builders, blacksmiths and machine-makers, glaziers, carpenters, colliers and plumbers. There was call for coachmen, carters and carriers, cartwrights and wheelwrights and woolsack makers, for wool buyers and cloth salesmen, and printers who also needed paper and printing machines. The mills had to have clerks, cleaners and porters.

The mill-owning, the middle classes, the managers and the merchant families required cooks, nannies and other household staff, as well as hairdressers, tailors, and gardeners.

Hundreds of factory workers needed butchers, bakers and greengrocers (who, in turn, needed farmers and market-gardeners), and drapers (they no longer had the time to produce food or to spin, weave and tailor for themselves). They would need cobblers and chemists, a few pubs, coal merchants, milkmen (relying on dairy farmers) and water-sellers, barbers, doctors and nurses, and, inevitably, undertakers. Some moved into new housing, closer to their work, creating employment for architects, builders and carpenters (although not much, at the time, for plumbers).

All members of the peripheral workforce created by the ever-expanding clothing industry needed the tools for their trade: toolmaking became another thriving endeavour, keeping the iron foundries busy. And the foundries and the mechanised mills needed coal.

In 1841 Bradford town boasted 83 worsted mills, 16 dyeworks, 250 warehouses, 40 collieries, and 22 quarries... and towering chimneys belching smoke over a population of 66,715. In the whole of West Riding there were 11,000 power looms at work; nine years later there would be more than 30,000.

Yorkshire Wool suddenly became the clothing product that everybody wanted, both at home and abroad. And, with some justification, the West Riding started to claim that 'We clothe the world!'

Beyond Bradford there were smaller factories creating and mixing new and traditional dyes, and tanneries making leather for pulleys and belts and, with wire from the steel works, equipment for scribbling and scouring.

More distant – although still inside West Yorkshire – Sheffield, Rotherham, Barnsley and Doncaster made the vital shears, scissors and other cutting tools, and glass, metal and pottery containers for dyes and chemicals for the wool mills, all items now required in far greater quantities.

But even within the heart of the Wool District, the old

tradition of one village being different from the next would prevail. Leeds also produced worsteds, Benjamin Gott creating a 'vertical mill' where everything – the scribbling and scouring, carding, fulling, spinning, weaving, dyeing, finishing and pressing – was integrated.

Leeds was also making progress with flax, raw material being imported from the Baltic via the Aire and Calder Navigation and spun and then experimentally woven into differing designs, weaves, colours, patterns and degrees of fineness and weight to appeal to different markets.

Halifax – another smoke-filled town (trees withered and died in the noxious fumes that filled the Calder Valley) – persisted with its kersey. And between 1841 and 1844 Crossleys built what would become an internationally famous mill for carpet-making at Dean Clough. It covered 20 acres – about the size of 10 football pitches – and, when steam-powered carpet looms were introduced, would employ more than 5,000 people, becoming the biggest concern of its kind in the world.

In Batley, Morley, Dewsbury and Ossett they produced mungo and shoddy, creating the recycling of waste and worn wool. They were following an invention by Benjamin Law, from Gomersal who opened Howley mill in Howden in 1813 to take in old wool clothes, tailors' off-cuts and rags and grind them back into fibre that could be re– spun into yarn and used again. Rags were also collected from households by carters – 'rag and bone men'.

Soft woollen clothes were used to make shoddy, the best of the recycled wools. Hard spun or felted products became mungo.

Wool cloth that had been woven with cotton or linen was subjected to treatment in hydrochloric or sulphuric acid and then after grinding produced a wool known as 'extract', an inferior wool that was exported to Europe in its raw state.

Originally used for padding, experiments to spin shoddy as a new type of cloth had produced material that looked at first like broadcloth but when tailored the gloss quickly wore off, exposing it as being inferior as clothing.

In 1828 a House of Lords committee was told that products such as clothing or carpets woven with shoddy alone were unacceptable. One retailer complained that 'when a broom is used upon it, it quickly wears out; they are goods made for sale, and not for wear'.

When blended with new wool shoddy produced a rougher cloth than that created by using only fine 'pure' wool, but it was of acceptable quality for inexpensive clothing. When woven onto a cotton warp, shoddy became known as 'union cloth'. It was cheap and became a favourite mixture for overcoats and uniforms.

Auction sales of rags were being held in Batley in the 1830s and in the 1850s there were weekly auctions of shoddy wool – evidence of a well- established and flourishing trade.

It was claimed that Benjamin Gott's mills did not use products originating from rags in any of their processes for the home market, although they did include cheap goods made from rags in the packages of textiles that they produced for export and sale to Native American tribespeople.

By 1860 Batley alone would be producing more than 7,000 tons of shoddy for spinning and there were 80 factories employing 550 people sorting rags for about 130 shoddy manufacturers.

That year the American census of manufacturers records the importing of six million pounds (about 2.7 tons) of shoddy which, according to another US government report, was used 'in the manufacture of army and navy cloths and blankets in the United States'.

Even inside Bradford township there was to be a degree of diversity. In 1836 Titus Salt discovered a practical use for alpaca and started working with a different type of wool; Samuel Cunliffe Lister started experimenting with the use of silk.

Railway Lines

With the advent of the railways, Leeds benefitted immediately with connections to London (change at Derby) and elsewhere via a variety of mainline and local fledgling railway companies.

Eventually, Leeds and Bradford had their own railway connection with stations between them at the wool townships of Stanningley (also handy for Farsley and Pudsey), Bramley and Armley, being served by the Leeds Bradford and Halifax Junction Railway.

One small obstacle was that Leeds to Halifax was not a direct line. Bradford could boast three railway stations – but they were not connected with each other. At Bradford (Wakefield Road) the train needed to back out to Laisterdyke and be shunted there onto another line to access the Halifax line via the suburban Bradford station at Low Moor.

The opening of the line may have been an auspicious occasion, but neither the unofficial nor the official first runs could be described as having had an auspicious start.

The line opened for business on Tuesday, August 1, 1854 and wool merchants were ready for it, having previously relied on getting their produce to Leeds on cart or on horseback. But the first train from Bradford was already 30 minutes late when leaving Stanningley. It was 50 minutes late arriving at Leeds Wellington Street station – geographically handy for the Cloth Hall but, alas, frustratingly late on that first day for the short hours of trading.

In the opposite direction, while third class fares for the five-mile journey from Stanningley to Leeds were 5d, from Leeds to Stanningley the fare was 6d. Trains from Leeds to Bradford did not stop at intermediate stations between 8.30 and 11.30 am – the first being too early and the second too late for manufacturers attending the Bradford cloth halls.

The formal opening of the line took place on the following day when a train comprising two second class carriages and a dozen first class carriages containing the directors, their friends and others, made the journey. The train left Leeds soon after midday and proceeded rather slowly, stopping at all the stations between Leeds and Low Moor and arriving at Bradford about 1.30 (ten miles in 90 minutes). Then it left Bradford shortly after 2pm, arriving at Halifax, seven miles away, about three o'clock.

The *Halifax Courier* (Saturday August 5) had its best descriptive writer on board…

> It started at Leeds Central Station and by a rather stiffish gradient reaches Armley. It has by this time obtained a considerable elevation, which it maintains until its junction at Bowling tunnel with the Halifax and Bradford line. It skirts the sides of the hills, passes through several very steep cuttings, over deep valleys by long embankments and cuts through Pudsey hill by a tunnel about a quarter of a mile in length. From its elevation occasional glimpses are caught of extensive landscapes. We pass populous towns and far and wide are

seen the evidence of man's industry for we are passing through the heart of the manufacturing district of the West riding. With a soil of no great fertility, with no apparent advantages in this locality are manufactories which have made the West riding fabrics famous over the world. The capabilities of this district are not to be found at first sight: they are to be sought and won and beneath the earth: all those exhaustless coal beds, and those valuable deposits of iron ore, which in the hands of the people unsurpassed for indomitable industry and energy have made this district one of the wonders of the world.

Between Leeds and Pudsey (which had no station yet) were halts at Armley, Bramley and Stanningley.

A short distance from this brings us to Laisterdyke, from whence on the right is seen Bradford and its torrents of smoke belching forth from legions of tall chimneys obscuring the glorious light of the sun and enveloping in a murky cloud all the country round.

At Laisterdyke the branch for Bradford diverges, the lines being here at a considerable elevation the approach to Bradford is a descent all the way, nearly a mile – the branch line terminates in the Wakefield Road where the station building is some hundred yards distant from the Lancashire and Yorkshire Railway.

Bradford will thus have three railway stations but all unconnected with each other.

Just after the arrival of the first train to Bradford 'an untoward event occurred which for a time marred the pleasure of the day.'

Some passengers were still sitting in the train but those on the platform watched an engine coming down the incline. It slowed down but failed to stop and hit the rear carriage of the celebratory train, throwing Miss Firth [daughter of the man in charge of the festivities] against the carriage window and causing –

'a violent contusion over the left temple which bled profusely. A gentleman standing in one of the carriages was thrown down and many of the ladies were terribly frightened, but we are glad to state that with the exception of Miss Firth no one was hurt.

After this brief excitement the train was shunted back to Laisterdyke and thence to Bowling station, where it joined the Halifax–Bradford line which it passed very slowly then dashed through the Bowling tunnel and drew up at Low Moor.

Another brief stay then it was back in motion 'at a steady pace' to arrive at Halifax station about 3 o'clock.

> The inhabitants had assembled in great numbers to welcome its arrival and the bells of the ancient parish church struck a merry peal. And the splendid band of the Second West drawn up on the platform welcomed the travelers with the strains of the national anthem.
>
> The mayor called for three cheers for the opening of the line which were given with right good will.

… As he should have done, considering the palaver involved in getting a train through from Leeds to Halifax in about three hours.

It was, in fact, not the improvement of the town's prominence, but the end of it. Getting there, only via changes and shunting at Bradford and Laisterdyke, was too much trouble and a waste of time. Bradford was far more accessible.

[Note: trains to Bradford from Leeds nowadays take an average time of 20 minutes; and to Halifax (direct, no changes) about 35 minutes. From Bradford to Halifax takes 12 minutes.]

Rise and Rise

Until the start of the 1800s, Bradford had simply not figured as a wool town in its own right. For most of its history it had been a coal town with a wool market serving the weaving villages around it. The goods were brought by the weavers and bought – 'in the white' by Leeds merchants who took them home for finishing.

Its commerce relied mainly on the use of inns and offices for traders who visited the town on account of its production of iron and coal, as much as for wool.

But, eventually, the enterprising burghers of Bradford woke from their comparative slumber and turned their hands to dyeing and cropping and finishing – and found that they were good at it. Enterprising manufacturers experimented with different types of wool mixing – and discovered that they worked. They found that they could, with a little applied ingenuity, adapt the cotton processes to steam powered weaving of wool, in all its forms and mixes. By the middle of the century it was full steam ahead – literally, for it was the railway that had clinched it.

The linking of Bradford with the Canal had greatly improved its communications. Ease of access was far further developed to the town's advantage when the railway brought Bradford almost on to the main line, more or less isolating Halifax which was then beyond the main arteries of traffic. The importance of Halifax – which, in any case, was by now concentrating more on Crossley carpets – lessened, and Bradford assumed the position of premiership in a booming worsted industry.

Bradford at work

Getting ideas above its stations (all three of them) the number of spinning mills had soared from one in 1800 to 130 before the first train steamed into Bradford amid the 'torrents of smoke belching forth from legions of tall chimneys'.

Trains now conveyed Bradford's products to Leeds and from there to all parts of the realm or to ports for shipping to the rest of the world. In the 1860s Lord Palmerston, the Prime Minister, laid the foundation stone for a magnificent Gothic revivalist building on a triangular site in the centre of town. This was to be Bradford Wool Exchange, a stunning edifice that would emphasise the importance and wealth of its wool trade and where its trading would be echoed throughout the world of wool.

By 1900 there would be 350 mills in the city, by which time two-thirds of the country's entire wool production was being processed in or around the borough.

Indeed, prior to 1914 Bradford was reckoned to be the wealthiest city in Europe, because of wool, and for the next half-century it would be said that there were more Rolls-Royce cars, per capita, in the Leeds-Bradford conurbation, than anywhere else in the world.

Obviously, though, the wealth was not evenly distributed among the area's citizens.

The Giants

Many new fabrics and machines used in the processing of wool were invented in Bradford and great fortunes were made by Victorian men. They, in turn, developed the town, building parks, houses and great halls. The fame, wealth and achievements of the mill owners were, and still are, legendary.

Titus Salt (1803-76), a mill-owner's son from Morley, had inherited his father's business and expanded it to the extent that, with five mills working, he was the biggest employer in Bradford and he believed that better working conditions would result in greater productivity.

He bought a greenfield site three miles outside town beside the River Aire and the Leeds and Liverpool Canal, and along the Bramley turnpike and the new Leeds to Bradford railway line, and on it built a giant new mill with its own village – 'Saltaire' – of airy houses (upwind of its chimneys) with running water and gas lighting and outside lavatories. There were public baths, parks, allotments, a school and a library, a hospital, alms houses, a church and a chapel, shops and an institute (but no alehouse) and he moved his workers into it. Then he introduced pensions for his employees as they retired.

Titus Salt

When he asked for a goods depot and a small station platform on the railway line he was refused, so he bought shares in the Midland Railway company and reapplied, this time successfully.

In 1836, having gone to Liverpool to buy imported wool, Salt had stumbled across unsold bales of Alpaca fleeces from South America.

He took samples back to Bradford to experiment with their spinning and weaving, then returned to the warehouse and bought the entire consignment, having discovered it to be remarkably lightweight, strong, lustrous, high in insulation value, and resistant to rain and snow. He created a highly fashionable new form of cloth for the British and overseas market.

When it opened in 1853, Salt's Mill was the biggest factory, of any industry, in the world, with 3,000 workers and 1,200 looms. Six storeys high, 180 yards long and spread over 11 acres, it produced 30,000 yards (more than 17 miles) of cloth every day.

The machinery was steam-driven, requiring 50 tons of coal every day, drawing water from the River Aire and the smoke passing through a 'fuel economiser' before belching out of a 250-foot chimney. Inside the mill was a reservoir of 500,000 gallons of water for wool washing, with a further 70,000 gallons in a tank in the roof in case of fire.

A dining hall, linked by a tunnel to the mill, would typically feed 600 workers with breakfast and 700 for dinner. Later developments included the mill's own dye works, and a gasholder that provided lighting for both the mill and the houses.

Salt's Mill was not, in fact, the first township of its kind in Yorkshire. In 1847 brothers Edward and Henry

Akroyd had built 132 terraced houses for their workers at Copley, in Calderdale, south of Halifax, along with allotments, a dining hall that would feed 600, a school, and a library.

Ten years after Saltaire had opened, Henry Ripley (1813-1882), boss of the massive Bowling Dye Works (with 1,000 workers, the largest in England), announced his own industrial model village – of 300 'workingmen's dwellings' with gardens at the front, yards at the back, plus allotments for growing food – on his own land in Broomfields, East Bowling. Only 194 were completed, along with a school, a teacher's house and, later a church. But all the houses had an internal WC – until then very much a middle class preserve and virtually unknown in working class dwellings.

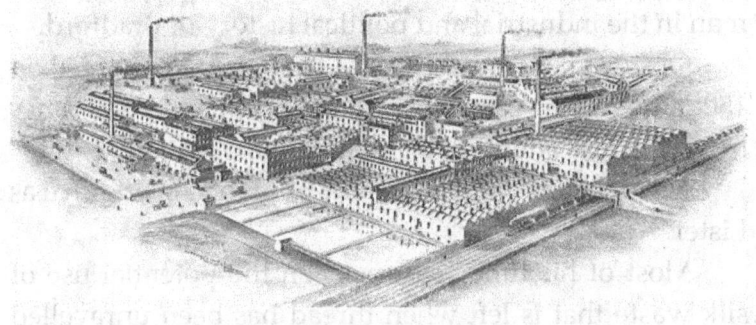

Despite his concern for the workers, Ripley, who was knighted as a Liberal MP and then ennobled as Baron Ripley of Rawdon, objected to dealing with the newly– formed dyers' union when it called a strike in 1880, stating that:

> 'Many of your grandfathers, fathers and sons have worked at Bowling all your lives and this is the first occasion on which you have, during a long series of years, ever assumed a hostile

> attitude. I appeal to you not to listen to the advances of men who really care nothing about you, and have not your real interests at heart.'
>
> (*Bradford Observer*, February 7, 1880).

National Census records for 1881 show him living at a house in Rawdon called Acacia, along with his wife Susan and 13 servants. He was a town councillor, a magistrate, chairman of the chamber of commerce, and one of the founders of the Yorkshire Penny Bank.

And then there was Samuel Lister (1815-1906), born at Calverley Hall, whose father had built a worsted mill for him in Manningham in 1838. It was the first in the area – although there were already 200 handloom weavers locally.

Lister may have been the single most important man in the industrial and political history of Bradford.

Obsessed by inventions – he patented more than 150 of them – he came close to bankruptcy several times by giving less attention to the mill than it required.

Few masters were as distant from their workforce as Lister.

Most of his time was spent on the potential use of silk waste that is left when thread has been unravelled from a cocoon. Eventually his efforts paid off with his invention of an appliance that enabled him to make good quality yarn at low cost. He imported silk waste – at about a halfpenny a pound – from India and China and turned it into yarn that he sold for 23 shillings a pound, to make poplins, plushes, velvets and carpets.

The last process to be modernised was wool combing. Raw wool needs to be separated and straightened before it can be spun into mixed worsted yarn, and it was a hot, dirty and tiring job that occupied thousands of people working in their own homes. Many attempts were made to build a machine that could comb wool mechanically, but none was successful until Lister bought up several failed patents and combined their best elements and improved them, thereby creating the 'Lister Nip Comb', and revolutionised the industry.

Samuel Lister

His combing machines came into such demand that though they cost only £200 to make he was able to sell them for £1,200, and the saving they effected in the cost of wool production brought about a reduction in the price of clothing, and the increase in sales created the necessity for new and better supplies of wool. The machine improved even the best long-fibred wool, and also the mohair, alpaca and cross-bred long English wools.

In 1845 he combed his first pound of Australian Merino, thus contributing to the development of Australian sheep farming.

His inventions made clothing permanently cheaper, bringing greater prosperity to Bradford.

Lister's profits were estimated at £250,000 a year in 1871 when fire destroyed the mill he had inherited. At this time he was the owner of nine wool mills – four others in England, another in Germany and three in France.

He built a replacement mill in Manningham in the Italianate style of Victorian architecture with floor space of 27 acres – the largest and most imposing textile building in the north of England. Railway wagons from the company's own mines at Featherstone, about two miles south-west of Pontefract, brought 1,000 tons of coal every week – 166 tons a day – to feed the mill's boilers.

High above them, and above the whole of the Bradford basin, towered a 249-feet tall chimney, fashioned in the manner of a Venetian campanile. The chimney, which alone added £10,000 to the building costs, stood – and stands today – as a proud boast of Bradford's manufacturing glory. Its height may have been a concession towards the anti-smoke activists: in 1868 Lister had been taken to court accused of smoke pollution from his previous mill and had been fined five pounds, plus costs.

He made few concessions, however, to his massive

workforce, which lived in cramped slum conditions on oatmeal diets while he planned a life in the fresher air of the north country and started buying adjoining estates around Masham, including Middleham Castle, Jervaulx and Swinton Park. He had made himself lord of a manor stretching from the outskirts of Ripon to the start of Wensleydale. When he was ennobled for services to industry (as well as for lavishly entertaining royalty and established nobility at coursing and shooting parties on his vast areas of land) he took the title Baron of Masham.

Panic

It might have been difficult, through all the smoke and soot and steam, to see it, but in the 1850s Bradford was the fastest developing town in the kingdom and was replacing Leeds as the perceived centre of the English wool industry. People started referring to English wool as Yorkshire wool, and then as Bradford wool – regardless of the part of the Riding, or of the Empire, from which it came.

From Hull to Moscow in the east, and from Liverpool to San Francisco in the west, it was Bradford cloth – in one or more of its local variations – that everybody wanted, and in which everybody, from princes to railway porters, was being dressed.

Its success appeared unstoppable. And so it would have been, were it not for changes in the world economy which would have a disastrous impact on the mills and their workers.

Neither contemporary commentators nor modern economic historians can agree about what caused a massive American financial crisis in 1857. It was not the first in that newly developing country (nor would it be the last). News of previous crises had been spread by travellers on carriages, stagecoaches, steamboats or mule trains. But, by 1857 telegraphy had been invented and information was instant. Bad news, as the saying goes, travels fast.

At this distance in time it probably does not matter so much about the cause of what would become known as 'The Panic of 1857', except that it was a confidence crisis that involved the failure of a massive trust and insurance company (Ohio Life), the end of the Crimean War, and excessive speculation in securities. This involved investors on both sides of the Atlantic, which produced uncertainty in the American economy and caused the first recession that would affect the entire known world. British investment in US industry – especially in its railroads – often using money borrowed from British banks, stopped, and then dropped in value.

What this meant to the wool industry was, firstly a drop in exports to (what had been) a growing American market where, now, 5,000 businesses were failing, and secondly, a withdrawal of the previously generous terms of credit that had been available to the mill–owners.

Clothing is usually an early victim of any financial contraction – presumably because most people, when money is tight, can manage for a while without new clothes. For similar reasons, it is also one of the first industries to recover at the end of a recession.

But it meant that wool workers were put on short time and then laid off, indefinitely.

The busiest, most productive and most thriving area of industrial success in England was suddenly awash with unemployed workers. Lancashire's cotton mills were suffering in the same way.

These were bleak times for the north.

From August 1851 to March 1862, Karl Marx worked as a correspondent and columnist, mainly for the *New York Daily Tribune* but also for any newspaper that would pay for his writing. Journalism provided Marx with a platform and a wide readership and was the only regular source of income he ever enjoyed.

In 1857 he wrote in the *London Free Press*:

> At least 5,000 persons, consisting of skilled artisans and their families, who get up each morning and know not where to get food to break their fast, have applied for relief to the Union, and as they come under the class of able-bodied paupers, the alternative is of either going to break stones at about four pence per day, or going into the house, where they are treated like prisoners, and where unhealthy and scanty food is given to them through a hole in the wall.

But men who worked intricately with silk and with the finest wool could not possibly expose their delicate hands to stone-breaking, Marx observed, so it was the poorhouse for them.

He continued:

> The present convulsion bears the character of an industrial crisis, and therefore strikes at the very roots of the national prosperity.

In a letter to his friend Friedrich Engels, whose father owned large textile factories in Salford, and in Barmen (Prussia), Marx wrote:

> Your information about conditions in Manchester is of the greatest interest to me, the newspapers having chosen to draw a veil over them.

In February 1858 he commented in the *Tribune* that:

> at the present moment the industrial crisis rages most violently in the British woollen districts, where failure follows upon failure, anxiously concealed from the general public by the London press.

Wool workers in the West Riding may not have been aware of Marx's writing, not even when it was published in London, but they did not need to be told about it.

When the mills had been at their most active and productive they had complained about the arduous work, harsh conditions, long hours and the low rates of pay: but the mill owners granted few concessions. They kept the different specialised units of the production process apart, so that, when complaints were raised, only one section of the workforce would be affected and represented. Compromises could therefore be granted to some small groups but not to others, thereby avoiding workers uniting in any proposed industrial action

This could not be the start of trade unionism, nor even of 'commune–ism'. If faced by any form of industrial disruption the owners threatened to respond by closing their mill. There would be little point in protesting or in threatening to withdraw labour from a factory that had shut down.

But the seeds were being sown...

The economic panic of 1857 was sharp, but short, with the mills reopening the following year. And with workers resuming their complaints about there being too much work but too little money.

The civic authorities in Bradford had been unprepared for the explosive growth of the town, from 29,800 in 1801 to 150,000, 50 years later. The population, most of it attracted by the prospect of jobs, existed in overcrowded houses with little access to clean water and lacking drainage, sanitation and ventilation. Disease and sickness was unavoidable.

Although Bradford was proud of its three railway stations (Leeds had only two), it would be another 50 years before Bradford could be considered as a civilised place to live with a clean supply of water, underground sewage, organised police and fire services, a slum clearance programme, street lighting, public baths and rubbish collection and plenty of grand Victorian architecture. By the time it achieved city status (in 1897) it could also boast of a new general hospital, libraries, public open land for recreation, and a (horse-drawn) tram service.

It had to work hard to keep pace with its neighbour, Leeds, which claimed, with justification, to be the Wool Capital of England (and therefore, naturally, of the entire world).

In 1858 about 500,000 people cheered the arrival of Queen Victoria as, accompanied by Prince Albert, she arrived to open Leeds Town Hall, designed to be the biggest in the country. It was erected on what was then the edge of the town centre, magnificent and impressive, to emphasise civic pride in the undisputed capital of regional industry. It had cost (the 2020 equivalent of) £13million, about three times the original estimate, at a time when its citizens were still suffering dire poverty.

In front of it was a 35-ft tall, 40-ft diameter, fountain which would be removed in 1905 and replaced by a statue of Queen Victoria. The fountain was re-erected in front of Elmfield House, at Town End in Bramley, and was connected to the boilers of Elmfield Mill, at the other side of Stanningley Road, so that Reuben Gaunt, the mill owner, knew when the engines were running.

Bradford opened its 'Wool Exchange' based on the Stock Exchange, in 1867.

Trading on the Exchange was by verbal contract only, each party keeping a separate note of the price, quantity and quality. Only members elected by the Committee were allowed on the trading floor, where many thousands of pounds changed hands – literally, on a handshake. For, in the Wool exchange, as in the Stock Exchange, a member's word was his bond.

There was a dress code: suits and hats (bowlers for merchants, trilbies for spinners and top hats for the millionaire mill–owners) were de rigueur.

Spinners stood by numbered columns in the hall of the building so that regular buyers could find them more easily.

Non–members, properly attired, could watch from a balcony and try to catch a member's eye and close a deal 'off floor'. However, 'off floor' trading between members and independent merchants was not guaranteed in the same way as the oral contracts between members who were subject to their code of honour. Non–members had to take a chance on the quality and price of the goods they were buying.

And, although a so-called 'Bradford Deal' was to be considered sacrosanct, all the purchase deals between members were subject to scrutiny by the Exchange which checked quality and weight before delivery – although nobody ever mentioned that fact..

Membership of the Exchange identified a person as being among the top tier of traders in the West Riding.

Because of diversity in the wool industry, figures for wages are difficult to quote precisely but it seems that in 1838 power-loom weavers were earning around 11s a week, about the same as the best handloom weavers, but the best power-loom men may have been on 13s.

In 1853 there was one weaver to each loom; in 1861 it was three looms to two weavers; and in 1873 two looms for one weaver.

By 1857 – some 30 years after the introduction of steam power – most weavers were young women. In 1886 there was one man for every ten women and there was littler differentiation of wages between the sexes. That year's *Wage Census* showed some highly skilled women earning as much as 17s 6d a week, although the average pay was around 13s for a 56½-hour week.

There are no records for home spinners, but the 1923 *Census* shows a spinner–overlooker (of maybe 40 children) on 22s; the children earned 2s at 12 years of age, increasing by 6d a year. Ten years later girls would outnumber boys, 11 to one. In 1857 most spinners in factories were 'women and young girls'. And by 1886 some overlookers were on 29 shillings a week.

However those figures can be no more than rough guidelines because not all of the Yorkshire mills had completed *Census* returns.

Sales of wool and worsteds reached what would be a peak figure for the century during 1870-74, earning £25,900,000. Wages rose too, and Bradford weavers would look back with both pride and regret on a short period when 20 shillings a week was considered a lowish wage, For there were lean years to come, and as the century was drawing to its close the region's seemingly inexorable economic growth would come to a stop again. Because of events in America... again.

Labour Relations

In December 1890, the United States imposed a new tariff on 'low quality' foreign cloth which translated as a general drop in profits throughout the British textile industry.

Samuel Lister's immediate solution to a potential falling of company profits – just after declaring an 8% end-of-year bonus for his shareholders – was to post a notice in his Manningham Mill announcing a cut in wages of 15% to 33% for 1,100 workers, mostly weavers. This was to start on Christmas Eve, along with the threat of a lock–out in the event of any opposition.

Worst–hit were to be the plush-velvet weavers. Although basically a worsted factory, Manningham had diversified under Lister's influence to silks and velvets. Disorganised though the workers may have been, this was too much for them and 5,000 of Lister's workforce, most of them not members of any form of union, downed tools in sympathy or were locked out by management.

What made the walk–out so dramatic was the size of it. Most Bradford mills of the time probably employed no more than 50 workers, while Manningham employed thousands and claimed to be the biggest silk mill in Europe. So ease of communication, possibly mixed with a growing feeling of comradeship, would result in a move towards workers communicating better and cooperating with each other.

Many of the strikers were, of course, women, some of whom were on lower rates than men doing the same jobs. On January 2, 1891 the *Manchester Guardian*, reporting a march through the streets, remarked that:

> 'One striking feature of the procession was the very large proportion of well-dressed women which it included.'

The West Riding Association of Weavers organised public meetings and a strike fund, for which collections were made. There were demonstrations in the streets and rallies in the Star Music Hall. A committee was set up to negotiate with the employers, even offering to accept a 5% cut in pay, but got nowhere. Nor was any help coming from the Liberal Party, from which they might have expected support.

Support came instead from workers in Colne Valley, Halifax, Huddersfield and Salford. Women who sewed the cloth from Lister's mills marched from Leeds to join the demonstrations. A reported 20,000 people attended a rally held in St George's Hall.

The Strike Committee issued 25,000 copies of its Manifesto

> 'In the face of these low wages we are of the opinion that we should be doing not only an injustice to ourselves but the whole of the textile industry in the West Riding of Yorkshire by accepting the proposed reduction... Help us fight against this enormous reduction. Our battle may be your battle in the immediate future.'

The appeal evoked a remarkable display of working-class solidarity. The Trades Council gave its unswerving support, as did all the Bradford unions, and the Yorkshire Miners' Association sent both money and speakers to Bradford. In the nineteen weeks of the strike £11,000 was collected.

In face of all this, Lister blustered. He brought 'strike-breakers' in – blackleg workers who could not make the machinery work efficiently. He threatened to close down the giant mill completely, and move all its work to one of his other mills, at Addingham.

He wrote that:

> 'The women spend their money on dress and the men on drink so that the begging box goes round. It matters not what wages are.'

...While Lister, any paternalism and philanthropy having flown out of the window, was spending his own money – the profits that his workforce had made for him – on buying up the North Riding. He could not have written a more effective manifesto for the activists if he had tried.

Nevertheless, by the end of April the Christmas strikers were worn out and worn down by hunger, hardship and the inability to pay their rents. According to the *Manchester Times* the majority of strikers had been 'without funds' from the start. They had been refused Poor Relief from Bradford Council on the basis that they were not out of work but refusing work.

In mid-April, four months into the dispute, 160 men of the Durham Light Infantry were summoned to break up a mass meeting and a fortnight later the strikers returned – beaten and bowed by hunger and a sense of futility – to work.

On the face of it, they had achieved nothing.

But the Manningham workers' defeat would in fact have several major consequences. Within a month of the strike ending, it had brought trades union organisers together as the Bradford Labour Union which, in turn, led to the creation, in 1892, of the Trade Union Congress (TUC) and then, to a conference held in Bradford in 1893, of the 'Independent Labour Party' (in that it was independent of either of the major political parties). Keir Hardie, George Bernard Shaw and Fred Jowett attended that meeting. The workers turned their backs on the mill–owning, church–going, and 'paternalistic' Liberal politicians who had given them little oral and no actual support. Thus, in 1900 the Labour Party was formed to represent the interests and needs of the urban working class.

Samuel Lister died at Swinton Park during the 1906 election – while people were still voting – without seeing the effect of his contribution to labour relations. Fred Jowett, a textile worker and the first socialist on Bradford City Council, became Labour MP for Bradford West, one of 29 Labour MPs elected that year.

Lord Masham had changed British political history.

The Manningham mill, however, went on without him, employing 11,000 men, women and children at its height, and proudly producing 1,000 yards of velvet for King George V's coronation in 1911.

Not every mill owner had reacted so strikingly to the American tariff, nor been so remote from his workers, as Samuel Lister. There was always, after all, the home market. Bradford Chamber of Commerce estimated that total quantities of wool, mohair, shoddy and other types of woven product had increased from 373 million pounds (weight) between 1865–9 to 685 million 30 years later, although they dropped in 1900–1904 to 659 million.

There was a market everywhere for good worsteds and an increase in exports to all corners of the globe. Hainsworth's, for example, was sending cloth worth £120 to £330 a month to its own agent in Rio de Janeiro.

Abimelech Hainsworth's grandson, AW or 'Young Bim', had bought Temperance Mill in Stanningley in 1882 and devoted it to worsted weaving. In 1889 it had ten worsted looms; in 1901 it had 80. English Worsted exports soared from 4.3 million yards in 1882–4 to 25.5 million yards in 1890–4.

Young Bim was a popular employer, known to treat his weavers to supper when work was slack, and he arranged outings from the smoky factory environment in which they lived to the fresher air of Southport, Scarborough or the Lake District. He also ensured his workers' health and welfare by subscribing to the Leeds General Infirmary and to the local 'Amicable Sick Club'.

Perhaps because mills were smaller than elsewhere and because the bosses were seen regularly on the shop floor, and although the general wage seemed hardly to change, there was surprisingly little trade union activity among the concentration of mills in Stanningley, Farsley and Bramley – the patch between Leeds and Bradford. A proposed 'mass meeting' of Pudsey, Farsley, Bramley and Stanningley textile workers in 1899 – eight years after the Manningham strike – attracted fewer than 20 people.

During the First World War workers were actually encouraged to join trades unions in order to give employees single bodies with which to negotiate strikes or 'working to rule'. Trade union membership was about 4 million before the war, and more than 8 million by the end of it.

Rise and Fall

The late 1880s and the 1890s saw a steady fall in wool prices. Merino wool exporting was no longer the sole preserve of Australian farmers – the wool was now also available from New Zealand and South Africa. Plentiful wool meant lower prices; lower prices meant less income, so sheep farmers were encouraged to experiment with diversification. They had all those sheep, but what about making a profit from their meat? England was already importing mutton and 'lamb' from the colonies, after all.

But it quickly transpired that, as George III had discovered, Merino meat (even though as lamb it is reportedly highly rated) was not acceptable to the British palate. The answer, then, fairly obviously, was to cross the Merino with a flock whose meat would be acceptable. The Australians, it may have appeared, had lost the plot and were shooting themselves in the foot..

Whether the mongrelised mutton turned out to be palatable or not, the wool sheared from an experimental cross–bred sheep for 14 years of its pre–abattoir life was going to be of inferior wool.

This did not phase the Yorkshire weavers because, for a start, it was cheaper still and, secondly, they could easily find use for cross-bred Merino wool. Not every customer required the world's finest wool for their clothing.

The cross-bred flocks accentuated the falling export price. The West Riding weavers were buying it all up. In some cases they did not even need to weave it: Germany was taking three-quarters of British yarn exports and, in 1895, 90% of Egypt's imported goods were British yarn. Some firms decided that there was more profit in spinning the wool than in processing it and gave up weaving altogether, at least as a temporary measure.

In 1899 there was a shortage of cloth.

The British Army, seemingly destined to be perpetually at war, kept many of Yorkshire's mills in business with orders for uniform and blanket cloth. But during the mid-1800s the pattern of warfare changed. Opposing troops no longer lined up in ranks, face-to-face, exchanging rifle fire by appointment. There were now spies or scouts, covertly creeping forward to spot and report on enemy positions. There were snipers, in hiding, picking off troops on the opposite side, and guides, invisible to the enemy, directing distant artillery fire. For most of the time Britain was now fighting, not in grassy hills and valleys in European fields but in dust or sand among rocks or in foliage, and mainly fighting in Africa or Asia. The once famous red coats were no longer appropriate.

During the 1860s soldiers in India switched to locally produced uniforms in khaki (from a Hindi word meaning 'soil-coloured'). With the outbreak of the Boer War in 1899 the first orders were received in Yorkshire for the new product: 'khaki serge, 56 inches wide, half-milled, with a worsted crossbred warp and a woollen weft' (versions of which are still worn by the British Army: in 1902, scarlet uniforms were redefined as being for ceremonial wear only).

Yorkshire mills could produce the required cloth in a standard and consistent dye – an amalgam of six different colour coordinates – until the outbreak of the Great War in 1914 when many thousands were required in a hurry which exposed a limited stock of dye. The dyers had then to confess that the true and acceptable khaki colour had actually been researched and created and made in, and sourced in and imported from... Germany. (The German army wore many different colours but generally favoured *feldgrau* – field grey).

English dyers frantically attempted to match a khaki from their own mixtures, with the result that the First World War started with Allied soldiers in an odd array of so-called 'khaki' hues – until the War Office called on the expertise of Leeds University's Department of Tinctorial Chemistry and Dyeing, to establish a consistent recipe.

[The other side of the coin was that officers in the Kaiser's navy – including the Kaiser himself – could no longer have their dress uniforms tailored in London from Yorkshire worsted. Such are the fortunes of war.]

Sales of uniform khaki – along with material for caps, shirts, gloves, and socks – peaked in 1915, a year that started with one million fighting men and would have almost two and a half million by December.

The War Office wanted to check both the quality

and the colour of the cloth being woven in the north, so demanded that individual bolts of it be sent to its London depot in Pimlico for inspection before being sent back by train (to Leeds) for tailoring into uniforms. When the industry pointed out that this was a time-wasting procedure for a production process in a hurry, the War Office commandeered the Leeds tram shed in Swinegate, and moved its inspectors there.

Posters started to appear in the streets, asking 'Why aren't you in khaki?'

Between 1901 and 1912 the value of wool cloth and yarn exports had almost doubled, achieving 54% of the world's wool trade between 1909 and 1913, but there had been a distinct downward trend in cloth sales in 1913.

In May, 1913. the *Halifax Courier* reported:

> Strikes and rumours of strikes fill the local atmosphere at the moment. There is general discontent in practically all organised trades with the wages prevailing which, it is contended, are insufficient to meet the increased cost of living. Some strikes have been in progress for weeks, one or two for only a short time, and others are threatened. Trades union organisations seem to be paying special attention to Halifax at the moment but the same spirit of unrest is also manifesting itself in other towns.

Pay was kept low and wool prices were high. Some spinning mills were working only one and a half days a week and in September 1914 some mills were reporting working at 'a definitive low'.

Nevertheless, when the War broke out Britain was the world's greatest trading nation. Its imports and exports were nearly a third larger than Germany's and 50% more than the United States'. For four years of war shipping from the UK was almost impossible, although not so in the oceans beyond Europe. While Britain could not satisfy the demand for wool (or cotton) to its colonies, or to America (North and South) or Asia, the USA nearly doubled its trade with Latin America, while Japan stepped up its textile exports to India, China, and the United States.

War work had meant employment for many but also a loss of skilled labour as men went off to fight for 'King and Country'. Typically, the male millworkers were outnumbered by women, two to one.

Khaki quality was worth less per yard than fine worsted cloth but one Stanningley firm, Hainsworth's, recorded monthly War Office orders that sometimes exceeded £7,000, whereas before the war an average might have been less than £1,500. In total, during the war, its mills produced 109 million yards (about 62,000 miles, equal to two-and-a-half times the circumference of the earth) of uniform 'drab' and 32 million yards of greatcoat cloth, in addition to an impressive 231 million yards (131,250 miles) of narrow flannel for shirts and hospital use.

In 1916 the *Wool Record* reported 'the greatest boom' of the British textile trade. It was a year in which 'all records for turnover, consumption and values have been broken.' In December of that year the government took control of the sale and purchase of all wool.

It demanded all the wool product from Australia and New Zealand, and brought South Africa into the same contract in 1917. These were, after all, Commonwealth members.

And in October 1917 army ordnance requisitioned four floors of the mill warehouse at Shaw Lodge in Halifax as a boot–repair depot (for which, eventually, the firm received compensation of £1,000).

The mills were increasing, and sometimes doubling, their number of workers in order to cope with demand. The price of wool had been set by the government at 15½d per pound in 1916 (more than 50 per cent higher than the average in 1914) and the War Office was buying cloth in bulk, at discount rates, but there were still profits to be made.

The Great War had coincidentally created a huge blow, from which the old industry would not fully recover.

From the start of inflation – in some instances up to 60% – following the armistice at the end of 1918 to the start of the Second World War in 1939, Britain remained a world leader in wool textile production. But, unable to recapture its export trade, had failed to expand, renew or refresh its business. Nor could it afford to keep pace with the depreciation of its machinery.

A familiar figure in the Wool Exchange at that time was Sir James Roberts, ninth of 11 children of a tenant farmer and part–time weaver, who had left school at 11 to work as a worsted spinner at Old Oxenthorpe Mill. He rose to become mill manager, then moved to Bradford to manage a spinning mill there, then went into business on his own – so successfully that, in 1892, at the age of 44, he bought into Salt's Mill and by 1900 was the owner of Saltaire, both the village and the mill.

Learning that Tsar Nicholas II had his own flock of Merino sheep, he travelled there to make a deal to buy the wool more cheaply than its price in the open English ports. He learnt the language and visited the country frequently, investing heavily and establishing beneficial deals.

The revolution of 1917 changed all that, seriously affecting Sir James' fortune. He had increased the size of Salt's Mill by about a third, and the number of employees from 3,000 to 4,000 by the time he sold the mill in 1918 as a going and thriving concern for £2 million.

Foreign markets lost during the war would never be regained. The home market remained strong but at the same time fashions were changing: shorter skirts and dresses, jackets and coats required less cloth and therefore fewer weavers.

The only bright spot on the horizon was when Coco Chanel introduced a sporty 'casual chic' style for women, using fine wool, and showing women that wool could be fashionable.

The 1920s were a volatile period with prices see-sawing between record highs and lows, and with adverse exchange rates, unsettled markets, slow paying customers all having consequences for the industry. And now that they were all dependant on steam, the mills were also affected by a series of coal miners' strikes.

Unemployment levels among textile workers – who were still clattering in iron-tipped clogs to work, where they could find it – reached more than 25 per cent in

1925–6, rose to 37 per cent in 1931 and remained at an average of 20 per cent between 1929 and 1939.

In 1928 the *Wool Record* reported:
> The annual production of raw material is insufficient to run all the machinery in all countries full time, but mill owners everywhere endeavour to keep their plants employed, hence in a period of trade stagnation, there is the inevitable price-cutting. Selling below cost may be condoned as an expedient to tide over temporary difficulties; continued indefinitely it can only lead to the bankruptcy court.

Having lost so much of its export market, weavers concentrated more on the home trade which, assisted by tariffs on cheap foreign imports, consumed three quarters of all woollen and worsted cloth by 1937.

Nevertheless, between 1919 and 1939 one third of Yorkshire's looms became redundant.

Worstedopolis

But then, once again, there was 'war work'. And, this time, Britain was ready for it. Until 1938 Germany had been an importer of wool from the UK and a competitor in textile production. But that year the countries of the Commonwealth were told to stop all forms of trading with Germany and a deal was done with the dominion's wool producers to buy their entire clip for the duration of the war, and for one year after it ended, at 10¾d per pound, about 2d above the going rate. In 1942 the price was raised to 12½d.

In April 1939 – five months before the war started – the government was ordering an increased amount of uniform cloth.

Well in advance of hostilities the government had decided that the distribution of wool would need to be regulated and two days before war was declared a 'Wool Control' was set up. The obvious place to base it appeared to be in Bradford which itself had three-quarters of all the machinery of the entre wool textile industry, 80 per cent of which was based within twenty miles of the city.

Within a couple of days, all wool in warehouses was transferred to its ownership for redistribution under licence from the Ministry of Supply. Bradford was now not only the major town for wool making: it also was the only place where weavers or weavers' merchants could buy wool.

After close inspection by hastily established wool committees in the dominions, samples were dispatched to Bradford for appraisement. Wool buyers were invited to view and order the consignments. It was a move that angered the wool auction houses in London, who traded 30 per cent of wool from the Commonwealth, but their complaints were ignored.

Even the price of shoddy was managed by the Wool Control.

Bradford was where power and jurisdiction had been placed.

It was, rightly and officially, 'Worstedopolis'.

Rationing was introduced from the beginning of November 1939, and, in the middle of 1940, severe restrictions were placed upon the purchase of wool for civilian clothing.

Single breasted suits replaced double–breasted, the turn–up on trousers was abolished, as were zipped flies (because the war effort needed metal). Lapels were narrowed, the number of jacket pockets was reduced. (Shirt flaps were also shortened and double cuffs were banned to reduce the call on cotton.)

Some weavers were able to source yarn for weaving and tailoring from France, outside the Control system. But that opportunity ended with the fall of France in June 1940.

It was boom time for some mills and doom for some others.

The labour force shrank as conscription for national service in the forces and more strategic industries took effect, almost halving in the industry between 1939-44. Within a short space of time, almost every aspect of the wool textile industry had come under the close control of the state. Under these conditions, many firms closed for business and never re-opened.

At the end of 1939 the British Army had 1.1million men – regulars and newly conscripted Territorial Army soldiers. In 1941 the number was 2.2million. By the end of the war more than 3 million men and women had served. They all needed uniforms, mostly in khaki.

The same cloth – in different colours – was required for the Royal Navy and the RAF (Hainsworth's has been credited with having invented the recipe for 'air force blue'). Then there were the civilian services: police and firemen, air raid wardens, ambulance drivers, Civil Defence, the WVS and the Women's Land Army, railway employees, tram drivers and conductors, postmen...

During World War Two the wool industry produced nearly 410 million items of uniform cloth.

Lister's factory, for example, produced 50 miles of khaki battledress, plus 1,330 miles of silk for parachutes.

Before the War, only 40 per cent of the Australian wool clip had gone to Britain; 41 per cent had gone to countries in mainland Europe. South Africa's biggest pre-war customer had been Germany. Buying up all the wool product of the Empire had created an enormous surplus in the UK by the time the war ended.

In June 1945, when the embargo on sales to the Axis and Axis-controlled countries expired, the Wool Control had a surplus of some 3,300 million lbs of wool.

According to *Wool Record*, between 1946 and 1951 the British wool textile industry prospered, achieving a record level of production. Britain sold more cloth abroad than the rest of the world put together. But it was not enough. Rationing of civilian clothing, limiting the amount that people could buy, lasted until 1949, and from that time the industry's downfall would be determined.

The writing was on the wall, and the Yorkshire textile industry would never recover.

In 1950, there were 1,120 woollen and worsted mills in West Yorkshire; but by 1967, 400 of them had closed. Although in 1988 there were 700 still working.

A century after its great invasion by British and German immigrants, Bradford was to welcome workers from more distant lands. Refugees came first, during and at the end of, the war. They were followed by an influx of workers from the Empire, notably from India and Pakistan, in response to the shortage created by a perceived post-war boom and the Labour government's ban on women working night shifts.

Asian men were prepared to work at night and additionally took on jobs that the local population did not want to do.

In 1960, Britain exported 28 million kg of wool but by 1990 this had dropped to less than 11 million kg, while a new and relentlessly rising market in Italy was now exporting 51 million kg and had become the world's largest exporter of wool.

The number of British wool textile workers – about 50% of them were women – had plummeted from 164,350 in 1949 to 22,400 in 1990.

Critics pointed to the lack of technical innovation and the failure to refresh old plant and machinery, to adapt to new fashions or to react to increasing competition from overseas, while failing to attract new markets from the Far East and the developing world.

In 1966, Japan took over from Britain as the world's largest importer of wool.

Worst of all, the industry had failed to recognise the challenge of the petrochemical–based 'new kids on the block' – the manufacturers of 'man-made-fibres'.

Or, as the *Daily Mirror* described (in 1967) the new synthetic competition: flocks of 'little transistorised sheep, gambolling across man-made moorland'.

PART TWO

A Prince of Wales check

George III was the first European monarch to dress in a relatively modest manner – without feeling the need to express his power and importance with elaborate clothing. His 'Windsor Uniform', which included some ('full dress') gold braid, for men's wear at court (which he wore himself), along with an 'undress' version that had no embellishment other than red collar and cuffs on a dark blue wool coat, became mandatory. The King and his family all wore the uniform, and so did members of court.

Just as the celebrated 'Regency era' — the reigns of the Georges III and IV at the turn into the 19th century – was pivotal in the recognition and promotion of Merino wool, so it was in the creation of what we might call 'modern clothing' or 'modern fashion'.

'Farmer George' had known enough about good cloth to notice and appreciate the quality of wool in the coat of his missionary vicar, the Rev Samuel Marsden, to receive and wear a similar coat himself, and to give the priest sheep from his own Merino flock to make more of the same. He also introduced a law to ban the import of silk and to increase the wearing of wool. And meanwhile his son had 'gifted' (although the penurious prince had, actually, 'sold') even more Merinos from the royal flock at Kew to Captain Macarthur with instructions to set up a whole new industry in Australia.

The Prince Regent's interest in Merino wool was more important than his father's. The Regency period was the first significant era of modern fashion and styling in clothing, set by the Prince, the future George IV, and greatly influenced by the famous dandy, George Bryan – or 'Beau' – Brummell (1778– 1840).

[Brummell, the arbiter of men's fashion during the Georgian–to–Regency era, would doubtless have been aware of the quality of Merino wool, but he had fallen out of favour with the Prince and retreated in exile to France before he would have had the chance to wear it.]

At the start of the 19th century, male 'style' (which means the fashion or style at court, or in the capital – there was no fashion or style elsewhere) tended towards both the elaborate and the flamboyant, a rainbow palette of silks, satins and velvets, with more ribbons than a maypole, topped with fantastically high white powdered wigs. Those leaders of fashion had been on the Grand Tour and been introduced to outrageous dressing by their Italian hosts. They had also become excited by their discovery of pasta.

As more sombre fashions surpassed them, they became known as the 'macaroni club'.

Brummell, on the other hand, was the 'dandy' – a man who 'who studies above everything to dress elegantly and fashionably' (OED). He was the style-setter, the judge and jury of what was fashionable.

The French and American revolutions had spread dissent that marked the decline of fancily dressed 'aristos' and the rise of the individual, far more plainly dressed, 'dandy'.

Thomas Carlyle (1795–1881) described the dandy as
'A clothes-wearing Man, a Man whose trade, office and existence consists in the wearing of Clothes. Every faculty of his soul, spirit, purse, and person is heroically consecrated to this one object, the wearing of Clothes wisely and well: so that the others dress to live, he lives to dress.'

For the new age of social mobility Brummell (*pictured left*) prescribed only the most elegant simplicity: so out went all that was potentially ostentatious and flamboyant, in favour of a near monochrome, masculine, look – dark blue coats of military wool, buff–coloured vest and trousers, white shirt, dark boots.

And then he had the trousers pulled out of the boots so that the cuff broke neatly on the bridge of the boot (as the well–trousered peasantry had been wearing them for years.)

What mattered most, Brummell decreed, was that male fashions should be tailored to fit the wearer. The cut and the quality were what defined a good suit of clothes – fitting the cloth, without embellishment.

In other words, less was more.

It may have been that Brummell was prescient in that the bulk of the English population had recognised the French revolution as the distinction between 'them and us', the high–living aristocracy versus the starving working class. Revolution was in the air in England, and the ridiculously high-wigged foppish 'macaroni' more than emphasised the difference between poverty and plenty.

Brummell's new and understated look dictated the style that well–dressed men still follow today.

A bronze statue commemorates him in Jermyn

Street, London, with his quote: 'To be truly elegant one should not be noticed'.

There may be some irony in the fact that Brummell was not only noticed, but copied. What he meant was that if people noticed the suit, there was something odd about it: what they should be looking at was the wearer.

Perhaps sadly, he would never have enjoyed the experience of wearing a coat like his sovereign's, in the new Merino wool. Equally sadly, perhaps, is that there is no record of the precise cloth that he did favour, because he frequently changed his tailor.

He said this was in order that none of them could therefore claim to be his 'personal' tailor, but it is more likely because his addiction to gambling meant that he was perpetually strapped for cash, while a gentleman could always get credit with a tailor, for at least one suit.

Nevertheless, Brummell's enormous influence had happily coincided with the age of the West Riding's recognition as the English – and as the European – wool centre. Fine English wool was the clothing of choice. And Yorkshire was where the King's coat came from.

Before the 19th century, the majority of clothes were bespoke, made either at home or by a professional tailor or dressmaker. Ready-made clothing was limited to uniforms, servants' liveries, simply-cut garments such as cloaks and smocks, accessories and sometimes second-hand clothes. Some tailors also carried small stocks of ready-made items, such as waistcoats, which were easy to fit. All that started to change in the 1830s.

Long before Queen Victoria made a fashion out of mourning clothes, Victorian gentlemen were wearing dark and sombre suits. In the 1850s men wore dark blue or black wool coats and trousers (sometimes grey), although waistcoats could be unmatched in a non-contrasting pattern or colour. It was a style popular up to the start of the 20th century.

Regency and Victorian periods were followed by the Edwardian, which generally was a time of great opulence, gaiety and frivolity both for men and women, directly inspired by the King (Edward VII 1901– 10) and his consort Queen Alexandra. Both were stylish and modern and thoughtful about the way they dressed. Prince Albert once remarked about his son (who would change his clothes several times a day) that:

> 'he took no interest in anything but clothes, even out shooting he was more concerned with his trousers than with the game'.

From the Prince Regent to the present day, Princes of Wales – our future kings – have been the leaders of men's tailoring style.

King Edward VII, while being Prince of Wales and heir apparent to the British throne for almost 60 years. was the trend–setter in men's style, being credited with the unfastened bottom button of a waistcoat (as his paunch expanded), front and back (rather than sideways) trouser creases, and trouser turn-ups.

He presided over a rival, and more lively, type of court than his mother's, 'the Victorian'. While all the people around the Queen were in mourning clothes, her son favoured 'morning' clothes, with a lighter look than the frockcoat that had been virtually an overcoat.

When, in 1865, as Prince of Wales, he wanted a more relaxed jacket than the restrictive and traditional tailcoat suit to wear at formal dinners he worked with Henry Poole of 15 Savile Row to create a shorter, tailless and more body-hugging suit. Poole's tailored it for him in 'celestial blue' worsted barathea.

While the court was in enforced mourning for Prince Albert, the jacket colour was changed to black or 'midnight blue' in the same material. It took time for even a future king's new fashion to catch on, but it would become ubiquitously known as the 'dinner jacket', and when it crossed the Atlantic, as the 'tuxedo'.

The first decade of the 20th century would also see the introduction of the lounge suit and the sports jacket.

Poole and Co had been the first tailors to open on 'the Row' – in 1846, 30 years after Beau Brummell had fled town to escape his creditors. Poole's clients list has also included King George V, the Tsar of Russia, the Shah of Persia, the Danish Royal Family, and the Crown Prince of Japan, as well as prime ministers Benjamin Disraeli and Winston Churchill.

At Number One Savile Row military tailors Gieves & Hawkes (Hawke had a royal warrant from George III), clothed the Duke of Wellington as well as Lord Nelson and Captain Bligh. They currently tailor for the Queen and Prince Charles, as they did for Prince Philip.

In the 1920s they were the first Savile Row tailors to make and (don't tell the neighbours) to sell ready-made suits that they could export world-wide.

Frederick Scholte (No 7) made suits for the Duke of Windsor (Edward VIII, from January to December, 1936) when he was Prince of Wales, and continued after his abdication, despite having flatly refused to make him a pair of fashionable Oxford bags in the 1920s.

When pushed, Scholte sold him the cloth so that he could have them made up in New York; it was, a procedure the Duke would follow until his death.

As Edward, Prince of Wales, he introduced what he called the 'soft look' to male fashion. He was passionate about texture and insisted on wearing British cloth. At only 5' 5" in height, his jacket waists were tailored high to elongate his legs, which in turn meant that he could carry off bold stripes and checks.

He popularised the fashion of zipped, rather than buttoned flies. He ordered belt loops, because he disliked braces. The left pocket of his trousers was cut wider, to accommodate his cigarette case.

During his visit to the United States in 1924, when

he was the most photographed man in the world, *Men's Wear* magazine reported: 'The average young man in America is more interested in the clothes of the Prince of Wales than in any other individual on earth.'

Churchill, in a suit made by Henry Poole & Co

Although his grandfather (Edward VII) had been the first to wear it, it was the Duke of Windsor who made what was to be called the 'Prince of Wales check' a must–have item in the male wardrobe. Three actors wore it as James Bond on screen, as did Steve McQueen in *The Thomas Crown Affair* (which had been described as the most stylish movie ever made).

Twenty–first century man, seeking the correct look for modern men's wear, need look no further than pictures of the current Prince of Wales, Prince Charles.

He is the modern setter of style for the well-dressed man, eschewing anything made of 'man-made fibres', in favour of wool – preferably Merino. He appears to have worn only two overcoats since 1988, one in 'camel' colour with two buttons, and a breast pocket: the other in tweed with three buttons, and two deep, patched pockets,. Both coats are double-breasted, with wide peak lapels.

Proper styles will endure.

His suits also have not changed, either – draped and double-breasted, two buttons, notched lapels, two pockets without flaps and with double vents at the back.

When he was voted in *GQ* magazine as one of the best–dressed men, he was reported as saying he 'took it very much as a vote for what can perhaps best be described as the classic and timeless look of British style'.

Ready-to-Wear

Yorkshire had the memory of exporting raw wool, only to see it imported, with the weaver's mark–up, as cloth. It had moved on to exporting cloth, and seen it sent back as clothing (that, probably, did not fit). They realised the ancient logic of using the material, as well as simply weaving it.

We know, if only from Norman surnames (*Tailleur* and *Tynctor*) that the conquerors of Hastings brought tailors and dyers with them, and that they were at work in Yorkshire in the 11th century. These crafts folk were most commonly known as 'linen-armourers' – they made the garments, often padded, to be worn close to the skin under armour to prevent it chafing. As their trade suggests, they used linen, but they would also have used wool, which was far easier to weave and dye as a single piece with arm–holes and a slit for the head, sometimes with detachable sleeves.

In 1100 King Henry I officially recognised 'taylors' in Oxford; a royal warrant was granted to the London Guild of Taylors and Linen Armourers in 1299. Guilds started seven–year apprenticeships in the art of cutting and sewing. Until the invention of the sewing machine, and its introduction into England in the mid-1800s, every stitch sewn had to be done by hand.

(It probably seems incredible, today, but it is also obvious that every single piece of clothing, anywhere in the world, had been hand-stitched by someone with a needle and thread.)

At the time worsteds were becoming pre-eminent in Yorkshire, the clothing customer had three choices: cut and sew for yourself from a piece of bought (or home-woven) cloth; buy ready-made clothes in the nearest size, or buy clothes to resew to something resembling a fit. All girls – and some boys – were taught sewing from an early age.

The logical place for tailoring was Leeds, already the long-established merchant centre of the linen, cotton and wool trade. Woven pieces, sold as unfinished in the cloth halls, were most frequently taken to Leeds to be finished. Some tailoring was already well established in the town, where 'master tailors' would sub-contract the sewing, of suits they had cut, to people who worked from home.

Ready-made suits, as we came to know them, were 'invented' by John Barron, who opened a wholesale factory in Leeds in 1856, and was soon employing 3,000 workers, with 2,000 sewing machines. By 1881 he had 20 factories.

Other clothiers followed his lead. And in one year – 1890 – 15,000 people tailored five million garments in Leeds. By 1911, the number of people employed in clothing production in Leeds had doubled.

Mass manufacturing of clothing was an industrial revolution in the West Riding.

Some of the credit for changing the system is also due to Joseph Hepworth, from Lindley, Huddersfield, who left school aged ten (in 1844) to work in George Walker's mill in Leeds. Twenty years later he set up as a tailor and by 1881 employed 500 people cutting and sewing men's three-piece suits, either at a factory in Wellington Street or working from home. In 1890 he employed 2,000, mostly women, at his new Providence Works factory on Clay Pit Lane, and had opened more than 100 high-street shops, selling directly to the public and by the end of the Great War the firm could justifiably claim to be the largest clothing manufacturer in England.

Much later on the scene, and then hot on Joseph Hepworth's heels for the business, would be Montague Burton (born Meshe Osinsky, in Lithuania in 1885) who had fled from the Russian pogroms at the age of 15 and arrived in England unable to speak the language. He set up as a pedlar, selling clothes bought from a wholesaler, and in 1906 started manufacturing made-to-measure 'bespoke wholesale' suits with a factory, Elmwood Mill, in Leeds. In 1913 he had five men's tailor's shops, then, by 1929, 400 shops, which made it the largest chain of tailoring outlets in the world. And when Sir Montague Burton died in 1952 there would be 616 shops.

Burton's customers would visit a shop, and if nothing ready made on a hanger suited or fitted them, they would inspect swatches of fabrics, have their measurements taken, place their order and pay a deposit. Their suit was then manufactured (made to measure, to the customer's specifications) in one of

Burton's Leeds factories, which might have been Concord Street Mills, Byron Street Mills or one of the other facilities on Woodhouse Lane, Melbourne Street or Millroyd Street.

There were other rivals – Alexandre the Tailor started with a market stall in Leeds in 1895 and in 1950 expanded overseas with the United States Army in Europe... Jackson the Tailor, opened in 1906 as a small shop in Clayton Street, Newcastle upon Tyne and expanded into a nationwide empire of 70 stores, before merging with Burton's in 1953... Dunn and Co (1887), specialising in tweed jackets, blazers and flannels, which had 130 shops and 500 staff when it closed in 1996... Henry Price, whose first shop in Silsden (between Skipton and Keighley), opened in 1907 with only three shirt collars in the window, developed into a business with 500 outlets and 12,000 staff, bought out to become John Collier's, 'the fifty-shilling tailor' and sold to Burtons in 1985... and the smaller Horne Brothers, with 37 outlets and a staff of 250, whose target market was professional men aged between 30 and 40, and which closed in 1993.

As Henry Price, charging '50 bob' (£2.50p, roughly the average wage for a working man between the Wars), as the basic cost of a man's suit remarked: 'I can halve my prices and double my sales.'

These tailors mainly made ready-to-wear suits, but they could also make them to measure, or with unfinished trouser and sleeve cuffs. Easier, and cheaper, the ready-made suits could be sent to alteration tailors who, within a day or two (sometimes within an hour or two), would adapt the ready–made suit to fit the customer who had longer, or shorter, arms or legs than the stock size.

At the top end of the market – better known for its bespoke tailoring than for ready–mades – was Austin Reed's with 120 stores and about 1,200 staff when it closed in 2016 after trading for 116 years. In 2020 and operating on–line, it was selling suits for £500 with its 'super–premium' made-to–measure range at an average of £2,500.

And even that was small beer when compared with the prices in Savile Row where a similar suit might cost about the same as a small family car.

Wherever the suits were measured, it can almost be guaranteed that they would be made of good Yorkshire wool, and tailored in the West Riding, and often altered by homeworking tailors in, or not far from, Leeds.

What is probably little known is that Savile Row tailors would, after measuring a customer and cutting the cloth – from one of the 28 surviving Yorkshire mills that they still patronise – often send the pieces by train to Leeds to be sewn together by the city's independent small tailors. Apprentices would cycle two-and-a-half miles to Kings Cross with brown paper parcels that they would hand to the guard of the train, who would pass them on to a member of the tailor's family at Leeds City station. Then, a day or so later would cycle back to the station to collect the finished suit.

From the end of the 19th century, through most of the 20th and in some cases into the 21st Leeds was doing more than making its own and trading its neighbour's cloth, it was turning cloth into clothing for both the home and the export markets. More than emphasising Bradford's claim that the West Riding 'clothed the world', it now also dressed it.

The times when both weaving and tailoring were guaranteed a steady flow of business were, of course, during the two World Wars when there was a sudden eruption in demand. Literally millions of uniforms were required in haste, not only for the forces but also for many other uniformed organisations.

Thousands of women were recruited to take over the jobs previously occupied by men who had been conscripted, including (in Leeds and Bradford) filling shell cases with explosives, but most of the 'factory girls' who were not involved in weaving were employed at sewing machines, where they made battledress blouses and trousers.

Officers who could afford to do so were expected, and, in some cases, required, to buy their own kit – shirt and tie, underwear, socks and gloves, cap, tunic and trousers – and they would order it from the best retail tailor within their means. Not only officers: the trade magazine *Tailor and Cutter* noted in December 1914 that 'even the ordinary soldier, if he is able, has resorted to buying his own uniform as the quality is superior.'

And at the end of both Wars there was a vast need for civilian clothing as the nation reverted to ordinary life.

Enter: the 'demob suit' (a term not in common use before 'demobilisation' at the end of World War II).

Burton's was the lead manufacturer for supplying

these outfits, fitting out servicemen and women as they left the armed forces. Or, when they did not fit, tailors would adjust them, or even tailor them from scratch. While some people claimed that they were swapping one uniform for another, demob suits were offered in a range of colours and patterns, or as sports jackets or blazers with flannels. Because the outfits were literally head-to-toe (a choice of cap or trilby hat and of black or brown shoes), a demob suit is said, and generally accepted, to be the origin of the expression 'the full Monty', meaning that absolutely everything was being supplied by Montague Burton's, who had made 25% of all uniform clothing during World War Two.

More than 75,000 suits, 'of the best wool available', were being tailored in 1945 – most of them by Burton's but some by other manufacturers including John Collier and Simpson's of Piccadilly.

The demand enabled Burton to take over the vast Hudson Road Mills in Leeds from the wholesale clothiers Albrecht & Albrecht. These were already said to be the largest clothing works in the world, and were greatly expanded by Burton.

The first canteen at Hudson Road Mills, built in 1922, could accommodate 1,000 at a sitting. In 1928 it could seat 4,000 workers, and by 1934, 8,000. It was, of course, the largest canteen in the world. By this time there were 10,000 employees at Hudson Road Mills and Burtons was the biggest employer in Leeds. As well as its mass catering the factory had rest rooms and a medical clinic with dentists and chiropodists on site. Recreation grounds were provided for sports in 1935.

In 1946 Burton bought the Peter Robinson chain of women's wear shops.

In its peak year, 1960, Burton's tailors cut and sewed an estimated 1,560,000 men's suits – 30,000 a week.

By this time customers could buy suits designed by top names. In 1959 Hardy Amies (14 Savile Row), the Queen's couturier, teamed up with Hepworth's to design men's ready–to–wear suits and is said to have made more impact on men's style than on women's, for which he was already famous. The suits were favoured by Patrick Macnee, as the fashionable John Steed in *The Avengers* TV series.

Yves Saint-Laurent and Pierre Cardin styled ready-to-wears: designed in Paris, fabric woven in Rev Samuel Marsden's home town, Farsley, and tailored in Leeds. Karl Lagerfeld won international fame for his fashions in Merino. These were not only male fashions; Merino was also the fabric of choice for 'the little black dress', V-neck jumpers and sweaters, and for ladies' suits.

But new designers wanted to work with new materials and mixtures. The 'wool–mark', signifying an all–wool product was being replaced by a label noting the percentages of wool and terylene, a popular form of plastic, nylon polyactide, (polyester) that could be made to have the appearance of wool.

And at the same time fashions were changing. Cotton and denim became fashionable; man-made fibres became fashionable – or, at least, acceptable

For a time anybody who appeared in public would be expected to wear a suit. But even conservative places such as advertising agencies and city banks allowed 'dress–down' Fridays… which soon evolved to every-day laxness.

In the 1950s there might have been a hundred tailors describing themselves as 'Savile Row tailors' – if they were only in the vicinity of it. By 1980 there were 50. Now they are about 20, buying wool from the 28 Yorkshire mills (in 1900 there were 300 mills in Bradford alone).

In 1974 Burton's opened Topshop, designed for 13 to 25-year-olds, and in 1978 became Topman, aimed at 'the more mature' customer.

But Burton's clothing production ceased in Leeds in 1981 and its factory was taken over by Centaur (50% wool, 50% polyester).

In 1981 Hepworth's bought the chain of Kendall's rainwear shops to develop a womenswear group of stores and called it Next. In 1984 it created Next for Men and by 1986 Hepworth's was simply 'Next'.

Despite the downswing in sales of all-wool, or wool and mohair, or wool and cashmere, development of better production techniques and machinery enabled the manufacture of higher quality garments and Leeds remained a centre for bespoke, superior tailoring. Some Savile Row tailors continued to have their suits sewn in the city. And independent tailors continued to measure, cut and sew hand–made suits with worsted cloth from Leeds, Bradford or Huddersfield. although the good tailors were becoming difficult to find.

At the end of 1980s, the Australian sheep flock numbered 172 million, 80 per cent of them Merino and the rest Merino crossbreeds. Difficult economic conditions and severe drought caused their numbers to fall to a low of 98 million head in 2004. Continuing drought conditions further depleted those numbers and in 2016–2017 an estimated 74.3 million sheep were shorn in Australia.

Seventy-five per cent is currently (2020) going to China, where it is being not only woven, but also designed and tailored. And, because of the way Chinese industry works, its products are cheap.

The impact of the English bespoke wool suit on the clothing market has, it has sadly to be admitted, now diminished.

Happily, there remains a contingent of wise people the world over which recognises that English weaving, combined with English tailoring, is the one enduring definition of quality clothing.

2020 Vision

By the start of the 21st century suits were becoming less popular, with experts in exporting predicting the future of the wool shipping trade as being 'not bright'. By 2020 wool was six times the price of cotton and seven times that of synthetic fibres. On top of that, working the wool into fabric was (is still) a labour-intensive industry.

The new competitor has become China, its buying 75% of Australia's wool, compares with the UK at roughly 5%. China's buying increased from 21million kg, worth A$64million (£36m), in the 1980s to 271million kg, worth A$2.76billion (£1,55bn) in 2017.

With the most optimistic forecast being that sales will not change much, sheep farmers are turning more towards cereal and cattle which, given the increased demand for food from an ever-increasing world-wide population, seems a safer bet.

2020 was a year overwhelmed by a pandemic that closed most industries and saw factory workers, mill hands and retail sales staff sent home.

At the end of the year there were only two vertical wool mills in the UK, both of them in Leeds.

Hainsworth's, established in 1783, in Stanningley and Farsley, can count seven generations living through recessions and depressions, good and bad exchange rates, wars, local rebellions and strikes as well as plagues, ancient and modern. It carries on; having made wool for the uniforms in the Charge of the Light Brigade, it still produces high-end scarlets for the Brigade of Guards and the Royal Family and finest worsteds for the well-dressed civilian.

Since 1837, bales of raw wool have been coming in one door at Abraham Moon's in Guiseley and emerging as the finest worsteds – Marino mixed with mohair or cashmere – and Yorkshire tweeds, for suiting and for flat caps and sports jackets, and for hard-wearing luxury woollens for covering furniture.

Hainsworth's and Moon's are perhaps the luckiest, or more likely the most inspirational, world-class mills.

All that remains of Thompson's Mills in Rawdon, where the first pieces of Merino wool had been woven, are the fine three-bedroom villas with cottage gardens and distant moorland views that were built for the use of foreign buyers from the continent.

Lister's Mill, once the largest silk mill in the world, and also the largest textile mill in the north of England, employing more than 11,000 men, women and children manufacturing high quality textiles, velvets and silk at its height, closed in 1999. Its 27 acres of floor space have since been converted into flats – although its 249-ft high chimney continues to dominate the Bradford skyline.

Saltaire, a 'model' township with more than 800 houses and 1,200 looms weaving 18 miles of cloth a day, ceased production in 1986. It is now a UNESCO World Heritage Site and an art gallery (with the world's largest collection of paintings by Bradford-born David

Hockney), a museum, restaurant, and arts centre.

Benjamin Gott's mill in Armley, in 1805 the largest wool factory in the world, closed in 1969 and is now the Leeds industrial museum. His mill at Bean Ing, later known as Park Mill, in 1792 the first wool factory in Leeds and the biggest in Yorkshire, was demolished in 1965. Park Mill site was occupied by the *Yorkshire Post* and *Yorkshire Evening Post* newspapers from 1970 to 2013 and there are now plans to build houses, flats and an hotel on it.

To Let – The Bradford Wool Exchange had had its days of glory.
(Telegraph & Argus)

The rising popularity of the telephone meant that sales of wool could be made distantly and immediately, replacing the need for either party to travel for a deal.

The Bradford Wool Exchange – once the only place in Britain where wool could be bought and sold, where thousands of pounds worth of deals, sales, that affected world markets, were guaranteed by a handshake, and where the *Yorkshire Post* had once stationed four full-time reporters to cover wool prices – has not seen trading since the 1960s. Having first become a flea market, attracting a different kind of customer looking for a bargain, it is now a Waterstones bookshop. And even local historians know more about the building's architecture than about what used to go on inside it.

Bowling Dyeworks in Bradford, in 1881 the largest dyeworks in the world, along with the 'model village', were demolished in 1970, and now only its alms-houses remain.

The magnificent Halifax Piece Hall, opened in 1779 and the only cloth hall building left standing in the UK, did not even survive the 1800s. Given to the town in 1871 it became a wholesale fish, fruit, game and vegetable market. It is now home to a collection of independent shops, cafés, bars with some museum spaces.

Sunny Bank Mill in Farsley, which had developed from a mill for fulling wool in 1257 and been founded as a textile mill in 1829, ceased production in 2008. It has recently been refashioned as a home for small businesses and studios for artists, potters, printers and jewellery makers. There is a massage parlour in the old mending rooms and a bespoke tailor in the spinning mill. And it also includes an art gallery and a factory archive and has provided studio space for TV programmes including *Emmerdale* and *Heartbeat*.

Crossley's, in 1860 the world's biggest carpet mill (across more than 18 acres) in a multi-storey granite building, was, with 5,000 workers, the biggest employer in Halifax. The mill closed in 1983 and the complex has been regenerated to house art galleries, a theatre, a restaurant, and several small business offices.

In its heyday the West Riding had an estimated quarter of a million men and women working in its mills, 70,000 in and around Bradford.

Today, there are a few thousand and Bradford is perhaps better known for the number and quality of its curry houses than for the cut of its cloth.

In 2020 the *Yorkshire Post* reported that:
> ...many mills have simply succumbed to decay. In Keighley, Low Mill is now in a dilapidated state. So too are Old Lane Mill in Halifax, Newsome Mills in Huddersfield, Bank Bottom Mill at Marsden and several old mills in Bradford...

Bank Bottom was once one of Yorkshire's biggest mills, covering 14 acres, and employing 1,900 people on 680 looms in the 1930s. But it closed in 2003 with the loss of 244 jobs,

What is to become of them?

Historic England reported in 2018 that across Yorkshire there were an estimated 1,350 redundant and under-used mill buildings with the capacity to deliver up to 27,000 homes and 150,000 jobs. The report suggested that, with intervention, they could be brought back into public use, providing a solution for local authorities who are currently struggling to find sites for development and housing.

More recently a feasibility study, commissioned by West Yorkshire Combined Authority and looking at a sample of ten historic sites to assess their potential, has found that with intervention and an initial investment of around £7.5m, these 10 sites alone could create 1,223 homes or 4,800 new jobs.

Rawson's Mill in Halifax was quoted as an example.

The building, acquired by the Rawson family in 1836, is listed by Historic England because it is the oldest and largest surviving example of a multi-storey, steam-powered, iron–framed textile mill in Halifax; it is probably also the best–preserved example for its date in Yorkshire.

It is reckoned that with a £3million investment it could produce nearly 140 homes.

Some mills have already found a second life.

Belle Vue Mills in Skipton, one of the earliest (1828) steam-powered spinning and worsted–weaving mills, now houses Craven District Council offices and high-class apartments. Bowling Green Mills in Bingley are home to Damart, and Gibson Mill near Hebden Bridge is a National Trust visitor centre and a showcase of sustainable technology.

In Leeds, Armley Mills is now a museum telling the

story of the Yorkshire textiles revolution, while Marshall's Mills are offices. Firth Street Mills and Larchfield Mills in Huddersfield have become part of the university.

Out at Linthwaite, Titanic Mill is now an eco–spa.

...And Craven Mills in Bramley, a former woollen mill, became a wine warehouse. Boyes and Helliwell, woollen and worsted blanket manufacturers, became a Wickes DIY centre...

As Historic England reported:

> England's textile mills, once the workshop of the world, were the original Northern Powerhouse. They're fundamental to the history, culture and landscape of northern England.

It is a sad story when you compare the industry with its heyday but it's not a totally unhappy one. The numbers have dwindled but there are still companies in Leeds, Bradford and Huddersfield producing some of the finest textile products in the world. In recent years, there has even been a minor renaissance but the wool industry as we perhaps knew it is now very much a niche market.

Some high-end producers are still determined to make wool work. Moon's, for example, has extended into soft furnishings and is the weaver of choice for such labels as Ralph Lauren, Dolce & Gabbana, Burberry and Paul Smith.

Hainsworth's wool covers the Woolsack in the House of Lords and its wall coverings, curtains and blankets can be found in Windsor Castle and the Vatican. Its speciality weaving covers snooker and pool tables all over the world, as well as the interiors of Rolls Royce cars. The mill provides the fabric for protective clothing for fire services from London to Sydney, and blazer and scarf material for educational establishments around the globe. It even provides the wherewithal for the manufacture of woollen coffins.

In the face of severe competition on many fronts, innovative thinking about the uses and development of wool continues. In New Zealand ambitious weavers are experimenting with a product of the Rev Samuel Marsden's original Merino wool and the fur of possums (which are considered a pest in that country). Described as a 'luxurious' mixture, it is hoped that it will attract a new market...

Possum and Merino, known as Perino: it may catch on.

A Personal Postscript

When there are 13 members of a family living in one house, the greatest desire for a young man is probably to get out of it, and find some form of recreation, or employment or amusement on evenings and weekends. For George Barker, an apprentice with Rolls-Royce between the wars, this meant drill and artillery practice with the TA (Territorial Army) on Mondays, snooker on Wednesdays, table tennis at the church youth club on Fridays, cricket or soccer on Saturdays, and church on Sundays.

There were no televisions, nor even any telephones. Lads who wanted to meet again made arrangements for their next rendezvous each time they parted.

George was a pretty useful footballer, good enough, at least, to be spotted by a scout and invited for a trial with Derby County. He was not selected. As the smartest (and tallest) member of the Royal Artillery Reserve in Derby, he was, however, selected by the army – to march in the 1937 coronation of the King,, Edward VIII.

He and his comrades were volunteers in the 2nd AA (Anti-Aircraft) Division, being trained in gunnery and searchlight roles. It had been the new King himself who had insisted that the reserve forces of the Army,

Navy and Air Force should be involved in the coronation parade.

The late King, George V, had celebrated his Silver Jubilee in 1935 and the British monarchy appeared more popular than ever. He had died in January 1936 and preparations for the coronation of his eldest son, Edward, started shortly afterwards. The proudest moment of George Barker's young life was when he had learnt, at the age of 19, that he had the distinction of being chosen to represent the reservists in the coronation procession.

This necessitated hours of extra drill at the Siddalls Road barracks because he, and the other selected part-timers, would be marching behind the immaculate Coldstream Guards.

Impressively, he and his fellow TA volunteers would be kitted out with a new uniform – Number One Dress – in all–wool dark blue barathea, the outfit normally worn only by officers (who paid for their dress uniforms) on ceremonial occasions

It meant nothing to George that the soft fine wool would be woven in a mill 80 miles away at Stanningley, a small industrial suburb between Leeds and Bradford, nor that this first made-to-measure suit would be tailored in Bramley, an adjoining township on the outskirts of Leeds.

The significance would be relevant to him later.

Far more important to him was that, in the interim, Harry Franz, wool textiles correspondent of the *Yorkshire Post* (a newspaper with which George was to become familiar, years later), had been talking to the

Bishop of Bradford and had learnt about the King's relationship with Mrs Wallis Simpson – a divorced American woman currently negotiating a divorce from her second husband – whom he was determined to marry... even, apparently, at the cost of rejecting the throne. Harry's editor, Arthur Mann, then spent two days mulling over the story, before deciding to publish it. The story appeared in the *Yorkshire Post* on December 3, 1936, as, without doubt, 'the Scoop of the Century' and Fleet Street could not ignore it.

Edward now had to decide between his love and his duty as king of the United Kingdom and the dominions of the British Commonwealth and Emperor of India. After discussions with government ministers and senior clergy, on December 11 he chose abdication in favour of 'the woman I love'.

A Yorkshire Evening Post vendor announcing the abdication

Calamity.

The coronation for which young George had been rehearsing on the regimental parade ground, and for which he was to have been dressed so finely, was suddenly cancelled. The peaked wool forage cap bearing the Royal Artillery cannon, and the motto *Ubique* ('Everywhere')... the high-collared tunic with grenades at the fastening... the well–fitting tapered trousers with a broad red stripe... the new boots that he had stamped endlessly on the regimental square and had honed, with a bone, to make them shine, and then polished and tirelessly re–polished, were not needed. He was told that he could keep his smart new uniform, cap, boots and all: it was now surplus to requirements.

But then, just as suddenly as it had been called off, the coronation assumed new life. The earls and bishops who had initiated preparations for the timing of Edward's coronation, realised that it was too late to change it. They felt obliged to stick to the announced schedule and arrange Edward's younger brother Bertie's crowning, on the same date. Bertie decided that he would become George VI, honouring his popular father. The other George was once again back to drilling, and to boot polishing, in preparation.

So he marched along The Mall both ways, between the Palace and Westminster Abbey, with solemnity and dignity and with immense pride, in the coronation of his King.

And there the story might have ended.

Except that the Reserve was called to arms during the Munich Crisis of 1938 (for the first two years of the war the Army depended on volunteers), with AA units manning their emergency positions around the most likely targets for enemy bombing within 24 hours, even though many did not yet have their full complement of men or equipment. That emergency lasted three weeks, and they were stood down after a month. In February 1939, the existing AA defences came under the control of a new Anti-Aircraft Command. In June a partial mobilisation of TA units was begun in a process known as 'couverture' (coverage) whereby each AA unit did a month's tour of duty, in rotation, to man selected gun and searchlight positions. On 24 August, ahead of the declaration of war, AA Command was fully mobilised at its war stations.

George Barker was no longer a reservist, nor a Rolls-Royce apprentice: he was now a full-time soldier, a gunner in HM Forces.

He hung his Number One uniform on a hook in the family home in Nottingham Road and returned to rough khaki serge and, because he had been trained before the war in searchlights and gunnery – although at that stage he had never heard a live shell fired – he was moved around the country, especially along the south coast, to pass on his experience.

Just after 9 pm on Friday 14 March 1941, around 40 German bombers took part in raids on Leeds and Bradford, dropping incendiaries followed by tons of high explosives over the two cities.

A bit too late, the Army command realised that this area – best generally (but inaccurately) known as the Heavy Woollen District – was crucially vital to the war effort. In addition to the mills that were working non-stop to produce cloth and the factories that were turning them into uniforms, dotted between and alongside them were engineering factories making tanks, Spitfire fighters and Lancaster bombers, and casting and filling bombs and shells.

The raid was not particularly successful for the Germans in that they missed most of the industrially important mills and factories. But they hit the railway station, the Leeds Town Hall and the market and about 5,000 houses were either destroyed or sustained substantial damage, and around 65 people were killed.

Owing to censorship and secrecy during the war, the press did not mention Leeds or Bradford by name after the raid, instead referring to them as 'Northeast inland towns.'

But George was posted there, and stationed at barracks in Bramley, a village effectively little more than a mile long but with 29 textile mills within its postal address, roughly half way between and easily accessible to well-placed gun sites in both Bradford and Leeds. The AA batteries would be ready and waiting if the Luftwaffe came back.

Neighbours were encouraged to invite members of the forces, separated from their families for the duration of the war, for 'home comfort' in the form of Sunday afternoon tea. Herbert Culver, a Great War veteran working at the Cohen engineering works where shells and bombs were filled with high explosives, lived with his wife Constance Evelyn, their two young daughters, Molly and Nancy, and one son, Leslie, who was serving with the Black Watch. They lived in a narrow three-storey semi-detached house backing on to the barracks and owned by Agnes Nora Boyes, wife of the owner of Hough End Mill (Boyes and Helliwell, blanket makers) in Bramley. The Culvers said they would gladly invite a soldier to tea and this was how young George met his wife to be. Apparently it was 'love at first sight' both for him and for Nancy.

This virtually completed the jigsaw. George's remit included defending both Cohen's factory and A W Hainsworth's mill, next door to it in Stanningley, where his fine barathea had been woven, and Town End Mill where Nancy (known as a button–hole wizard) worked, half a mile from home, tailoring trousers for the forces in both high–quality barathea and khaki serge. The couple became engaged and from his next trip back home to Derby George returned with his dress uniform and hung it in Leslie's wardrobe in the attic of the Scarborough Terrace, Bramley, home.

It would be worn in its original configuration only once more – on George and Nancy's wedding day. At the end of the war Nancy removed the brass buttons and military insignia (including the broad red stripe down the trouser seams) and re–tailored it as a smart woollen navy blue jacket with matching trousers: for in Leeds tailoring only three pieces – including a waistcoat or 'a vest' – were deemed to comprise 'a suit'.

Their only son worked as a reporter on the *Yorkshire Evening Post* and the *Yorkshire Post*.

Glossary

Alpaca: Long, fine silky fibre with characteristics of both wool and hair derived from the Alpaca animal of South America.

Angora: Fibre from the coat of the long–haired Angora rabbit. Soft, silky and easily dyeable, it is distinct from the Angora goat, which produces 'mohair'.

Animal Fibres: General term for wool and hair, cashmere, mohair etc.

Bale: A package of wool in a standard wool pack for shipment. The common farm bale weighs between 200 and 450 lbs.

Barathea: an expensive fine English cloth, mainly used for uniforms or dinner suits. It is tightly woven with a slight diagonal weave appearance and broken rib effect and has a granular or pebbled surface but feels smooth to the touch.

Blanket: Cloth named after the man who first used it as a covering for warmth and sleeping purposes. Thomas Blanket (Blanquette), was a Flemish weaver who lived in England in the 14th century.

Bradford Spinning: English method of spinning wool into worsted yarn. The wool is thoroughly oiled before it is combed, producing a smooth, lustrous yarn. (As distinct from the 'French' system where the wool is spun in a dry state.)

Branding: Marking sheep, often with tar on the fleece, to help identify the ownership of the flock on open moorland, which adds weight to the fleece. Or stencilling on bales of wool to signify the owner, serial number, and type of wool in the bale.

Break: A temporary interference with the growth of the fibre, causing thinning and weakness of all or part of the fleece, caused by a sudden change of pasture, lack of feed or water, sickness, difficult birth, or faulty dipping.

Broadcloth: Compactly woven, elegant cloth with smooth nap, velvet–like hand and high lustre. It used to mean a cloth about

54 inches wide, but nowadays describes a fine form of cloth.

Brocade: Richly decorative fabric often made from coloured silks and may include gold or silver threads.

Brussels lace: Handmade lace made in or around Brussels, produced from the 1500s onwards.

Burling: In the dry finishing department of a woollen or worsted mill, it is the removal of undesirable matter from the wool.

Carding: Where a handful of short fleece was held on one flat 'card' (usually of wood or leather, with short nails or metal spikes in it) and roughly separated by pulling with another (something resembling a modern dog brush), until the tangled fibres produced webs that would merge for spinning,

Carpet Wools: Very strong or coarse wool types, generally hairy.

Cashmere: (1) Very soft, fine fibre, from the Kashmir or Pashmina goats of India. It is one of the finest animal fibres known. (2) Fine worsted dress fabric.

Clip: Wool from a given flock; also, total yearly production.

Cloth: Any woven fabric. In the wool industry it defines woollens as distinct from 'stuff' which is worsteds.

Clothing Wool: Sound, dense wool not more than one and a half inches, fine in quality, with an even crimp and good felting properties; used in the woollen trade.

Coarse: Wool that is thick in fibre diameter and also rough and inferior.

Combing: A step that is subsequent to carding in worsted spinning which separates the long, choice desirable fibres from the neps and shorter stock (noils), removes almost all foreign matter, short fibres, broken ends, tangled ends, and larger vegetable particles and arranges fibres in parallel order forming a sliver. Combed yarns are finer, cleaner, more lustrous and stronger than carded yarns.

Combing Wool: Wool suitable for combing on British and/or Continental type machinery; it should be sound and of appropriate length for the type. Fibres of wool from 0.5 to 6 inches long are used in worsted yarn.

Crimp: A natural waviness in an individual lock of fibre. In general, the closer the waves are together, the finer the wool.

Damask: a rich, heavy silk or linen fabric with a pattern woven into it, used for table linen and upholstery.

Dye: (verb) Colour wool by dipping and soaking.

Dyed-in-the-wool: When the yarn is dyed before spinning. as distinct from being dyed after weaving, or 'dyed in the cloth'.

Ell: An English cubit, the length of a man's forearm from his elbow to his middle finger. Two ells would therefore be just a little more than a yard: roughly equal to a metre and as wide as an upright loom could be in order for a weaver standing in front of it to pass the weft in its spool from hand to hand. [In later, Tudor, years the ell would be re-standardised to mean six times the span of a man's hand – then about 45 inches in England, but 37 in Scotland.]

Felt: An ancient technique that produces a non-woven sheet of matted material which is most frequently made from wool, hair or fur created by the entanglement of a mass of fibres that takes place when heat, moisture and pressure are combined.

Fleece: The coat of the sheep often removed as one piece.

Fulling: A primary process to clean a fleece and remove grease (lanolin) and then a finishing process in which the woven or knitted cloth is subjected to moisture, heat, friction and beating, causing it to shrink considerably in both directions and become compact and solid. It is said to be the hardest job in the cloth-making process. In heavily fulled fabrics both the weave and the yarn are obscured,

Greasy wool: Wool as shorn from the sheep and which therefore has not been washed or otherwise cleaned.

Haberject: A cloth of mixed raw colour, favoured by monks in medieval times.

Hank (English Worsted): 512 meters or 560 yards of worsted yarn. The count or size of the yarn is determined by the number of standard hanks that it takes to weigh one pound.

In the grease: Shearing sheep with unwashed wool. Wool used to be washed on the sheep's back before being shorn. Since the introduction of machine shears sheep are shorn 'in the grease'.

Knitting: Forming a single yarn into fabric of interlocking loops.

Lanolin: Wool grease; a secretion from the sebaceous glands of the sheep.

Linen: Fabric made from flax. Also refers generally to an item of underwear worn next to the skin, such as a shift or chemise as well as drawers, pantaloons or bloomers.

Loom: A device or machine for weaving cloth.

Merino: A very fine, soft wool from the Merino sheep. The breed of sheep.

Mohair: Fibre from the Angora goat, durable and resilient and known for its high lustre and sheen.

Mungo: An even more inferior product than shoddy, from heavy waste or felted cloth. The name is believed to derive from the rule that it must not go (in dialect, *mun't go*) in with any other wool process.

Nap or Pile: Ends of fibres raised from the body of the yarn that gives the cloth a fibrous surface.

Noils: Short, tangled and broken fibres, removed from wool during combing. Noils may contain vegetable matter. Used in the woollen and felt trade.

Piece-dying: Dyeing of fabrics in the piece after weaving or knitting.

Plush: Originally worsted with mohair or silk with the pile longer and less dense than velvet. mostly used for upholstery and furniture. (From Old French *peluche* = to peel, pluck).

Raw Wool: The fleece shorn from the sheep.

Recovery: The ability of a yarn or fibre to return to its original crimped state after being released from a tensile force.

Saye: A woollen blanket or military cloak of fine texture.

Scouring and Scribbling: Segments separated into differentiated grades (according to the part of the sheep) had to be hand washed in a tub to remove some of the muck, twigs, burrs, urine stains, dead skin, and grease that had accumulated on the sheep's coat after living for a year in the wild. This washing needed to be done gently so that it didn't further tangle or mat.

Selvedge: The edge of a woven fabric that prevents its

unravelling. (From Middle English: self + edge.).

Shoddy: Inferior quality yarn or fabric made from the shredded fibre of waste woollen cloth or clippings. The word (unrelated to clothing) came to mean badly made or of poor quality and it is believed to derive from the Old English for 'shed', meaning cast off, as in an animal shedding hair or a fleece. Outside the West Riding its real meaning has been forgotten (if it were ever known).

Shallon: A light, tightly woven worsted, a style of weaving in Châlons-sur-Marne (now Châlons-en-Champagne) introduced to England by the Normans.

Shrinkage: A reduction in length or width of a material caused by certain treatments, especially washing. A loss of weight and volume of wool due to scouring when grease, sweat, and foreign matter are removed.

Skirting: Removing the stained, unusable, or undesirable end portions of a fleece

Sliver or **Roving**: A form into which carded wool is processed. Wool is drawn through a tube that rolls the wool together and pulled out. This helps the fibres become parallel to one another.

Sorting: Separating a fleece or fibre into groups of comparable character and quality.

Spinning: The production of yarn. The twisting of the sliver or roving. The entire process of making yarn from fibre and winding it onto a bobbin or spool.

Spinning count: the number of hanks of yarn that can be spun from a pound of wool. The more hanks that can be spun, the finer the wool.

Staple length: The length of sheared locks obtained by measuring the natural staple without stretching or disturbing the crimp. Usually a year's growth equals approximately ten centimetres.

Stuff: Any form of worsted textiles.

Tammy: A coarse mixture of cotton and worsted. A cloth originally used for sieving wet food (French *tamis* = sieve).

Textile: Woven or knitted fabric.

Vertical Mill: One controlling every stage of cloth production from raw wool to finished product including Dyeing, Blending, Carding, Spinning, Warping, Weaving, and Finishing. Only two (Hainsworth's and Moon's) exist today.

Warp: the parallel lines of wool through which the weft is woven.

Weaving: Making cloth by interlacing yarns at right angles according to a predetermined pattern.

Weft: The threads which run from side to side of a piece of cloth. at right-angles to the warp.

Wool: Traditionally, the fibres covering the skin of a sheep but includes angora goat, cashmere goat, and specialty fibres of alpaca, llama, vicuna, and guanaco. Not 'fur' or 'hair'.

Structurally wool is crimped (has waves, folds or ridges), is elastic (can be stretched or twisted and returns back into place when released) and has microscopic barbs or scales on the surface of the fibre which allows strands to hook together.

Wool Sorting: Grading of fleeces and pieces into lots, each of which contains one quality only.

Woollen spinning: In this system, fibre is carded two or three times in different directions and goes directly from cards to the spinning process. Generally wool fibres used for this system are shorter, have more crimp and better felting qualities. The fibres in the yarn do not lie parallel to each other. With this system it is possible to use wools of different types, lengths and character together in blends.

Worsted describes the yarn (not a different type of weaving) and the product.

Worsted spinning is a system of yarn production designed for medium or longer wools, and other fibres. The suitable fibre lengths vary from 2.5 to 7 inches. These yarns are compact, smooth and more even and stronger than similar yarns spun using the woollen system. Worsteds are used for suitings and clear-finish tailored types of material. Worsteds hold their shape better than woollens.

Woven: Fabrics produced by interlacing yarns.

Yarn: A continuous strand of textile fibres that may be composed of endless filaments or shorter fibres twisted or otherwise held together.

www.ingramcontent.com/pod-product-compliance
Lightning Source LLC
Chambersburg PA
CBHW011343090426
42743CB00019B/3423